THE PENNY COLLECTOR

*How everything you do
is like money in the bank.*

STEPHEN S. NAZARIAN

Stephen S. Nazarian

12/2/15

For my grandma Winifred Nazarian.

Who, more than anyone, knew the value of a penny.

Stephen S. Nazarian

Contents

THE PENNY COLLECTOR

Stephen S. Nazarian

INTRODUCTION

I have always been a storyteller. In my adult life I have enjoyed recounting my experiences and adventures in both an accurate, and entertaining manner, but it didn't start out that way.

My first experience with school was attending the Penfield Village Nursery School in Penfield, NY. I was three years old.

I remember sitting in a circle on the floor, with maybe a dozen other three-year-olds. The teacher had us describing things about our homes. Some kids talked about their bedrooms, while others talked about pets, and things like swing sets in the yard. When they got to me I started describing our swimming pool in great detail, including the fact that it was forty-feet-deep.

Of course our pool was not forty-feet-deep. It was in fact zero feet deep, because we did not have a pool. I would not be the owner of any kind of swimming pool until 2002, three decades later. All that said, I think I really sold the story, except perhaps for the overstated depth.

When my parents went to their conference with the teacher, they learned about my tendency to exaggerate. Up to that point, the teacher actually thought we did have a pool, she had only doubted my grasp on what a reasonable depth might be.

EVEN BACK THEN, I COULD TELL A STORY.

This book is a collection of fifty-three stories, the majority of which I have experienced (at least somewhat) first hand.

The first story is called ***The Penny Collector*** and it is the setup for the remaining fifty-two. Each of the stories carries a message, an idea, a notion you can apply to your own life.

Why fifty-three? The Penny Collector story (as you will soon find out) is the inspiration for the subtitle of the book: *How everything you do is like money in the bank*; so that is chapter zero.

It is my hope that you will use this book as a guide to look at the things in your life from a new perspective. Read chapter zero, and then find twenty minutes, the same twenty minutes every week. During this time, read the next chapter, think about it, and then try and apply the message to the week ahead. The fifty-two chapters will last you one year.

I did not write this book to change people, or to solve their problems. I wrote it to tell entertaining stories anyone can use to, well, make things better.

I have no idea what better looks like to you, but I can promise you that if you slow down, find the twenty minutes a week, and really think about how each story applies to you and your life, you will be happier for the effort. I promise.

I don't care if you read the whole thing at once, and in fact it might be fun to do so. However, I've packed a lot into these 250+ pages, so when you're done, go back, find the twenty minutes each week and re-read it over the coming year.

I've also built a community at **thepennycollector.com** where you can go to share your own stories, communicate with other readers and get stuff. Some of the stuff is free and some of it costs a little, but all of it will enhance the effectiveness of experiencing this book.

I talk about a wide range of topics in the following pages, but indulge me in a quick aside on religion. I am not here to tell you what ***God*** should mean to you. I know what it means to me and it is very personal. That said I am neither shy nor reserved when it comes to talking about my own beliefs and experiences. My hope is what I have created here will enhance your own spiritual journey, whatever that might look like.

This book did not start out as a book. In early 2014 I started publishing a blog at **stevenazarian.com** with the subtitle of *Answers Hiding In Plain Sight*. The loose theme of the blog was "creative problem solving." Over the course of several months I wrote north of one hundred thousand words.

One day a friend of mine suggested that I turn some of what I'd written into a book and the rest, as they say, is history.

Writing for me is as important as exercising and nutrition, so if you like what you read here, fear not there will be more. Until then, I hope you enjoy the fifty-three stories on the pages ahead.

As for me, I'm going to take a dip in my really deep swimming pool.

0 – THE PENNY COLLECTOR

I was a Suzuki violin kid. From the beginning of first grade through the end of sixth, I took lessons, practiced with my mom, and participated in recitals. If you're unfamiliar, the Suzuki method of string instruction uses techniques that young kids can grasp easily without the need to read music. The program is broken down into a series of ten books that take years to get through. In six years I think I got through five of them.

Every time I started a new book, I would always do the same thing. I would flip to the back of the book to see just how hard it was going to get. On the first day of a new book, the beginning was supposed to be a stretch, but the end of the book looked nearly impossible.

Here's the thing, by the time you went to the lessons, received the instruction and guidance, put in the hours and pushed through the pages; the music and the end of the book was completely playable.

In the spring of 1987, I was one of the captains of the Penfield High School spring track team in Penfield NY. We had enjoyed a successful season of meets, and heading into the sectional championships we had a good chance at a team win. There were a few other teams that could win too, so if victory was to be ours it was going to be close.

Anyone who has ever been a competitive runner knows that training and talent are together only about 50% of the challenge.

THE REST IS THE HARD PART... AND IT IS ALL IN YOUR HEAD.

If you believe you can win, you have a chance, and you've put in the miles, and the conditions are right, you might actually be the first one across the line. However, if even one small part of you believes you will lose; you will.

*MENTAL DEFEAT IS LIKE A FLAME AND A PIECE
OF NEWSPAPER, ONCE IT CATCHES, IT TAKES OVER
IMMEDIATELY AND DESTROYS EVERYTHING.*

In running, winning does matter, but if you can step back and look at the big picture, it is actually just you and the clock out there. When you run an event faster than last time, that is a victory no matter what anyone else does. That's the theory, of course reality it is not that simple.

As a co-captain, a senior, and someone who really wanted our team to win, I struggled to come up with a way to inspire everyone to do their best. I needed them believe that they individually (and we as a team) could win. The sectional meet was on a Saturday in late May, and on the Friday before, I came up with a plan.

The 1987 Penfield Chiefs Boys Spring Track Team (see if you can pick me out)

Friday afternoon between school and practice, I walked down to the bank in the center of town and traded a dollar bill for two rolls of pennies. When I got home from practice that evening, I went down into the basement and drilled a quarter-inch hole through each of the 100 pennies. The next morning I asked the coach if I could talk to the team as we rode the bus to the meet. He said, "You're their captain, go for it."

I stood up at the front of the bus (behind the white line of course), and turned to face the bus full of kids. I handed a bag of pennies to each side of the bus and asked them to take one each and pass them back. I cleared my throat and said the following:

Today, you are each getting a penny. By itself it isn't special, in fact in 1987 there is nothing I know of that you can buy with just one penny. You need at least five of them to buy one piece of Bazooka gum.

But think about this:

Every day we get up and eat well. We go to school and exercise our minds. We come to practice, we stretch, we run distance and we stretch some more. We do weights, we run intervals and we compete twice a week. At the end of each day, we rest. In spring track alone, we've been doing all these things since early March. Each thing we've done to be better students, healthier athletes and stronger runners is like getting a penny. Every day for weeks now you have been collecting pennies, and today is the day we go shopping. I plan on spending everything I've earned and I hope you do too.

Each penny has a hole in it. I want you to unlace one of your spikes and thread the lace through the penny and put it down by the toe. Before each race today I want you to look down at that penny and say to yourself "let's go shopping."

I honestly don't remember if we won the sectional title that year. I suppose there is someplace on the Internet I could look that up, but it didn't matter. By the looks on their faces, I knew that my team was about to unload everything they had, and that was more than enough for me. I remember my two-mile relay team won, and we went to states the next week, but I don't remember if our team came out on top or not.

About ten years later I was living in New York City, but on a trip home I ran into an old track teammate at the mall. After chatting for a few minutes, he looked at me and said, "Hey, check this out." He reached down and pulled up the cuff of his jeans off the laces of his running shoes. There, at the bottom of the laces, down by the toe was the penny. After looking down, we both looked up and he said, "I've probably owned twenty pairs of running shoes since you gave that speech, and that penny has taken a ride on every pair."

I HAD HOPED TO INSPIRE MY TEAM FOR A DAY.
I HAD NO IDEA HOW FAR IT WOULD GO.

In the spring of 2003, my wife Emily had just finished her training and was about to start her new job as an Intensive Care Pediatrician. She was understandably nervous. "What if I kill someone?" she fretted. I didn't know what to say, but I did know she had been studying, training and preparing for years, and that she was ready. I thought for a moment and then I asked her to sit still for three minutes. I ran down to my workshop, quickly drilled a penny, grabbed a piece of copper wire and went back upstairs. I asked for her ID badge.

As I looped the wire through the hole in the penny and the clip of her badge, I told her the story of the track team and that bus ride back in 1987. To this day, that penny hangs off her ID, reminding her that no matter what she faces in the hospital, "she's got this."

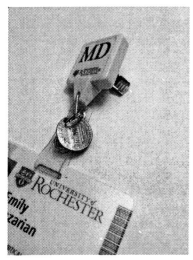

The penny on the ID badge where it still lives

We all struggle with confidence either globally or in little pockets. But, unless you are in a place where you truly don't belong, chances are you are more than prepared for whatever comes your way.

Has anything ever turned out even one-tenth as bad as you thought it might? No, I didn't think so.

Reach in your pocket or dig around in the couch. Do what you must, but find a penny. Take a good look at it and put it in the place where you experience your greatest crises of confidence.

Whenever it is "go time," look at that penny, think about all your hard work, close your eyes and say to yourself, "let's go shopping!" I promise you'll be happy with your purchases.

So now you've begun. Chapter zero is behind you and fifty-two stories lie ahead. If you want to soldier on and read through them all, go ahead, but be sure to carve out that twenty minutes a week. If you'd prefer to remain surprised each week you can do that too.

Either way, your year of penny collecting begins, now!

---

1 – THE DAY I GOT IN TOUCH WITH MY INNER TUBE

I love Independence Day. Christmas is a fine holiday for sure, and Thanksgiving has its positive attributes, but from the time I was about eight years old, the Fourth of July has been my favorite.

Maybe it's the idea that all Americans have the same stake in the celebration, or the fact that each year, my parents granted me a little more personal independence, but make no mistake – parades, picnics and fireworks served up in the early July heat are my idea of a good time.

Over the years, the standard Penfield New York Independence day has been made up of some combination of the following:

- Early morning race of some kind
- Late morning or early afternoon parade
- Late afternoon into early evening picnic
- Evening activities at Harris Whalen Park
- 10:00pm Fireworks on the hill

For several years there was a four-mile running race called the "Four For Fun." It never really caught on and eventually died off in the face of more popular races in neighboring towns.

When I was eight or nine, I was allowed to ride my bike with my friends to the parade, but we still met up with my parents and sat in the same place. However, there is something about controlling your own comings and goings, which makes you feel much more grown up.

When it was time to go to the park each year after dinner, my parents would establish a base camp up on the hill, and then we'd be released to frolic among the booths, food vendors and other entertainment in the lower part of the park. There are typically 20,000 people in the park, so to be allowed to roam around unaccompanied was a really big deal. We were expected back at the family blanket on the hill before they turned out the lights and then… fireworks!

When I got a little older, we used to get up before sunrise on the Fifth of July, and ride our bikes back to the park. When 20,000 people gather in one place in the dark they drop stuff; good stuff. Additionally, we would look for dud fireworks, or as they say call them in the military, "unexploded ordinance."

In 1979, the Penfield Recreation Department announced that there would be a race on the morning of the Fourth of July. It would not be a running race, oh no, they were planning a half mile inner-tube race on Irondequoit creek.

To say the least I was excited. This struck me as something I might be really good at, and certainly an event for which I could properly prepare. Some of my friends from the neighborhood agreed to race with me, and we all began making a plan.

I DECIDED THAT I NEEDED TO DO MORE THAN JUST FLOAT DOWN STREAM WITH A SINGLE TUBE, SO I SAT DOWN WITH A PENCIL AND GOT TO WORK.

I took two inner tubes and lashed them onto the top and bottom of a piece of plywood. Once that was complete, I cut another piece of wood in the shape of a rudder and attached to the back of the plywood platform with a hinge from an old cupboard door.

When my friends and I gathered on July Third to make our final arrangements, it was clear that I done the most work. Tim Buzby, one of the friends prepping for the race said:

"Either Nazarian is going to crash and burn or whip us all, I guess we'll find out soon enough."

David and Mike Sauter and Tim Buzby, all of Penfield, splash their way toward the finish line in the Irondequoit inner tube race.

Picture of my friends as it appeared in the paper

The day of the race came, and we piled into our respective station wagons to drive down to the creek. The start line was back behind the Oldsmobile dealership, and before we got into the water, I was interviewed by a newspaper reporter.

The reporter asked all kinds of questions about

my vessel and my plan, and as I descended the bank into the chilly water I was convinced that victory was soon to be mine.

THEN, IN A MOMENT, EVERYTHING CHANGED.

We all stood, holding our tubes against the current when the starting pistol was fired. Before any of us could move two, tall, skinny high school kids shot down the side of the creek, with bicycle tubes slung over their shoulders. Within the first minute I tore off my rudder and the rest of the race was combination of painfully slow floating, and even more painful carrying of the contraption I had so lovingly built.

Here's the thing; since "local creek inner tube racing" doesn't exactly have a national governing body, the rules are a bit loose. In fact if memory serves, the rules of the race may have been as simple as "participants will race ½ mile down the creek using inner tubes."

If that was the case, the two clever teenagers were certainly within the letter of the law. Whether they adhered to the spirit of the law was a subjective call nobody was willing to make, though you did have to admire their ingenuity. I don't remember what place I came in, but I do remember going home feeling both disappointed and a little cheated.

THAT WAS THE LAST TIME PENFIELD STAGED AN INNER TUBE RACE ON THE CREEK.

The next day I awoke to the newspaper sitting on the kitchen table. In the wake of the disaster the race had become, I completely forgot about being interviewed.

While writing this story I visited the Rochester Public Library to sift through reels of microfilm looking for the article. When I walked into the "local history room" I didn't remember what year all this had happened, but I did know that day I was looking for was July 5th, so it didn't take too long.

The reporter did a fine job of balancing the efforts of the twenty-five legitimate tubers and the surprise arrival of the two teenaged runners. My favorite part of the article was the place where the reporter described the scene as the gun went off:

"They bolted off, forcing everyone else to follow suit, including young Nazarian, whose craft was a sorry load to carry."

I learned several things that day, but if I had to narrow it down to one, it would be this. In every situation in life, there are some things you can anticipate and some that you cannot. For the things you cannot, sometimes your circumstances allow you to adapt, and sometimes they do not.

There is a scene in the 1981 movie *Body Heat*, where a character played by Mickey Rourke is discussing arson with the character played by William Hurt. Rourke says to Hurt:

> "Any time you try a decent crime you've got fifty ways you can mess it up. If you can think of twenty-five of them then you're a genius... and you ain't no genius."

I don't know if I was a ten-year-old genius or not, but that day was my first lesson in realizing that you can never be prepared for more than half of the variables in any situation. The best you can hope for sometimes is the knowledge that surprises are always just up the creek.

For the week ahead, don't limit your attention to only the things you know. As you sit in a meeting or have a conversation, pay close attention to both what is being said, but also what is not being said. Set aside time and resources for the unexpected. Think of it like the shoulder on a road. Most of the time you don't need it, but when you need it you really need it.

If you plan your day expecting some things to go wrong, you'll have that extra margin should it be necessary. Even better, on those days when everything goes according to plan, all the extra time you'll have will make it feel like your birthday. And who doesn't want that?

---

2 – COINCIDENCE? I THINK NOT

One Sunday our church bulletin listed a bunch of puns, and quips on the cover. Most of them were amusing, but one of them (similar to a quote from Albert Einstein) really stuck with me.

"COINCIDENCE IS WHEN GOD CHOOSES TO REMAIN ANONYMOUS."

If you chose to skip the introduction of this book, please go back and at least read the "quick aside on religion," found on page 10.

Back in the 1980s, my brother Doug liked to design running shoes. He had a handful of years as a competitive runner under his belt, and with that came ideas about how to improve the shoes on which he ran.

At the time, only a few companies were dedicated to running shoes and within each brand, the selection was a fraction of what we have today. Nike was one of the major players in the running game, having been founded by runners, for runners.

So, it was completely logical that if my shoe-designing brother was going to submit his ideas to a company, Nike was the best place to start.

I have no idea if his ideas were any good, but I do remember he used to sketch on graph paper using a fountain pen and a highlighter. Perhaps a bit unconventional, but his design drawings looked like nothing I'd ever seen before (or since for that matter). He got his hands on an address at Nike, and made several unsolicited submissions.

I DON'T THINK HE HAD A PARTICULAR GOAL IN MIND OTHER THAN NEEDING TO SEND HIS CREATIONS TO SOMEONE WHO MIGHT RECOGNIZE HIS GENIUS.

Months transpired, and to make sure they paid attention, he continued to send follow-ups of his ever-improving designs.

Around this time, Doug returned from college for the summer and had a job working at a downtown bank in Rochester. Sometimes he took the bus and other times he drove one of my parents' cars and parked at our church.

One day he drove the family Ford Pinto to work. Later that afternoon, I was sitting at home and I heard the telltale on-again, off-again moan of the mail delivery Jeep. I walked down the driveway to retrieve the family mail.

As I flipped through the stack of legitimate correspondence, mixed with equal parts junk mail and bills – I saw it.

Addressed to "Mr. Douglas Nazarian" was a single, white #10 envelope with a very clean royal blue return address that read "Nike, Beaverton OR." It would have been easy to simply put the mail down and wait for my brother to return home at the end of the day, but I had nothing better to do that afternoon so I decided to take the bus downtown to surprise him with the envelope.

I arrived at his office about half an hour before quitting time. He opened the envelope. It was a very polite letter thanking him for all of his submissions along with an explanation about how they didn't need any design help. However, they did describe a program where runners got to test new designs, and they were inviting him to be a part of it.

Not exactly what he had hoped for, but it was something. This however is not the point of the story.

After he finished with work, we walked the four blocks from his office to where the car was parked at the church, only to find one the tires in a state of extreme flatness. My brother is brilliant in many ways, but he has no mechanical skills whatsoever.

WE LIKE TO SAY HE HAS ONE TOOL IN HIS TOOLBOX,
A CREDIT CARD.

I immediately popped the hatch, grabbed the spare and the jack and began changing the tire. As I worked, our pastor came out of the building on his way home. Doug explained the situation, and how I just happened to take the bus downtown with the letter. He noted what a fortunate coincidence it was since he had no idea how to change a tire.

THE PASTOR SMILED AT US BOTH AND SAID, "THERE IS NO SUCH THING
AS COINCIDENCE," HE THEN TURNED, QUIETLY WALKED TO HIS CAR AND
DROVE AWAY.

In the summer of 1995 I had a good problem. I had accrued a chunk of time off, but I lacked the resources to go on a proper vacation. I knew I needed to get out of town for a mental recharge, so after weighing the few options I had, I planned a trip from where I lived in northern New Jersey to the home of my Godmother in West Burlington Iowa – 960 miles away.

Gas at the time was around a $1.00 a gallon and my little Saturn SL1 got thirty-five miles to the gallon, so the trip would only cost me about $30 each way plus tolls. The plan was to drive out in a single day, spend five days with my Godmother and her family on their ranch, and then return via Pennsylvania, spending the last weekend of the trip with my then girlfriend and her family.

Sixteen hours alone in the car gives you a lot of time to think, and since I was already leaning towards breaking up with the girlfriend, the drive to Iowa pretty much solidified what I had been considering for some time. I had a fine time in Iowa, but the entire time I was dreading the drive to PA, and the weekend that would follow.

On my drive back, I crossed the Mississippi river and the entirety of Illinois. I then transected Indiana, Ohio, and a bit of West Virginia, before crossing into the "Keystone State." I drove along the Pennsylvania Turnpike with Pittsburgh to the north, and then into a few hours of PA wilderness.

By this time I had consumed all my books on tape and I was completely sick of the CDs I had packed. Knowing what I was driving towards at 65 miles an hour, I was in a bad mood and generally not feeling too good about life. Five miles into Pennsylvania, a truck had kicked up a golf ball sized rock and put a solid crack in my windshield. Could things get any worse?

I drove through the darkness with my left hand on the wheel and my right hand resting on the shifter; my right index finger poking the "seek" button on the FM radio desperately seeking something to pry me out of my funk.

All of a sudden, there it was. It was 9:30pm and I heard the unmistakable opening music to an episode of *Seinfeld*. It was the one where Jerry used the black & white cookie as a metaphor for racial harmony.

The answer to society's ills, perhaps?

For exactly thirty minutes, my FM radio played the audio from a Pittsburgh TV station, making me laugh and yanking both my head, and my heart right out of the emotional rut in which they had been stuck. As the closing credits played, the signal cut to static just as quickly as it had appeared.

How is this possible? Well, back before HDTV and everything went digital, channels 2-6 in the US television system (called NTSC) overlapped with part of the FM radio dial. Look it up, it's true.

This all makes complete scientific sense except for one thing. Long before the show began at 9:30, I had driven out of range of any station transmitting from Pittsburgh. You could probably come up with some technical explanation about mountains, and signals bouncing off clouds at just the right altitude, but as the show ended, and with it my maudlin mood, I could only think of one thing: the voice of our pastor walking away from me and my brother that day in the parking lot.

We all go through our days experiencing good luck, bad breaks and "coincidences" that shape our lives. The sizes of these evens are infinite in range, but if we take a little time to think about "what just happened," we might see something more.

Think about the two or three most significant "coincidences" in your life, and how you were changed, even just a little. Then think about the idea of someone or something watching over your life; a force that has both your best interest at heart, and the ability to "make things happen."

For the next seven days, look critically at anything you encounter that could be thought of as a coincidence. Open your mind to the idea that there may be forces stronger than mere randomness in the universe.

You can call it God, karma, fate or intelligent design. I'm not telling you what to think; I'm simply saying that if you take the time to do so, you just might see something more.

---

3 – THE POWER OF THE CLIPBOARD

In the 9th grade I joined the Penfield High School Radio Club. There wasn't an actual radio station, but rather a bunch of DJ gear in a room about 100 yards down the hall from the junior-senior cafeteria where there was a pair of speakers on the wall. Those of us spinning records (yes, we used

The 1986 Penfield High School Radio Club – The end of an era

records) could not see nor hear the audience, so it felt like we were running a radio station; but in the end it was just the upperclassmen wolfing down starchy, greasy, food covered in government cheese.

I was part of the radio club from 9th – 11th grade, holding down a period-a-week DJ slot, but when we all arrived for our senior year, we were dismayed to discover that our beloved radio station had been converted into an academic office. All of our gear was disconnected and stacked up in a closet.

It wasn't the loss of the DJ opportunity that bummed us out as much as the deathly hush that hung like a fog over the cafeteria. The music had been pretty bad (it was the 1980s after all), but it was better than silence.

After chatting with Vice Principal Sullivan (the faculty adviser of the now defunct radio club), I secured permission to hook up enough equipment so we could listen to the local classic-rock station (96.5 WCMF) in the cafeteria. I also obtained permission from the lunch ladies, to put the equipment on a shelf in one of their closets.

So with permissions in hand, I went to get the job done. I dragged a school desk into the hall outside the lunch-lady closet, climbed up and removed a ceiling tile. I found the speaker wires that ran to the old radio room, pulled down eight-feet of wire and cut them. I then re-routed the now cut wires into the closet and hooked up the tunes. Easy-peasy right? Yes, but hold that thought.

Where I went to college, (Lehigh University) the only football game that really mattered was the annual game against Lafayette College on the Saturday before Thanksgiving. This is in fact the most-played college rivalry in US history (sorry Yale/Harvard). When the game was at home, tradition held that the goalposts be replaced with temporary ones made of painted 2x4s. At the end of the game, fans would stream onto the field and tear down the goalposts. The objective was to obtain the largest piece of goalpost possible, and display it proudly.

When I was a freshman, the game was at home in historic Taylor Stadium, but this year would be different. Taylor Stadium was being replaced with a brand new facility on the other side of the mountain and this was the very last game ever to be played on its hallowed pitch. On this day we all knew, much more than goalposts would be torn down.

As it turned out, the day of the game was cold – cold enough to freeze the foam in the beer cups held by everyone of legal drinking age. After a little tailgating, my friends and I decided to watch the game from the heated comfort of our dorm.

WE WON THE GAME 17-10, BUT THAT IS NOT WHAT I REMEMBER MOST CLEARLY.

The post-game demolition was impressive. Everything in that stadium that wasn't securely attached left in the hands of an exuberant fan. Signs, railings, toilet seats, they picked that stadium clean. I later heard that one fraternity (known for a concentration of electrical engineers) walked off with a pretty good pile of broadcast equipment that the TV crews had failed to clear before the game ended. It was mayhem.

Watching this on TV from our dorm made us all feel like maybe we had just missed something important, but being Lehigh students, this would not be the end of the story.

The Taylor Stadium Scoreboard... before

The next day was still cold, but sunny. My friend Stu and I decided to walk down to the stadium to see if the greedy masses had left anything. All we were hoping for was a chunk of concrete or something small like that. As Stu and I wandered the bare stands looking for anything of value, we both looked up at the same time and saw something too good to be true.

Perched on a steel structure above the main entry archway was the scoreboard. Upon closer inspection, it looked like the "HOME" and "GUESTS" signs on the scoreboard were removable. Game on!

Stu and I climbed up the back of the scoreboard, leaned over the top and removed 12 screws from each sign, and proudly headed back to our dorm with our bounty in hand. The scoreboard was not at all stable, and had we fallen, it was a damn long way down to the concrete below. Lucky for us, we were invincible eighteen-year-olds at the time.

What do these two stories have to do with each other? In both cases I was doing something that should have alarmed any passers-by, but in both cases it didn't.

As I was standing on a desk in the hallway of my high school, my head in the ceiling cutting wires, several teachers and one administrator walked by, and none of them said anything.

As Stu and I were on top of the scoreboard in broad daylight, campus police drove by twice on the road below and looked right up at us. As we were finishing up, a maintenance worker appeared at the other end of the football field and actually waved at us.

The "liberated" HOME sign as it hangs in my basement

25

Furthermore, we learned a few days later that some other students, having seen what we had removed from the scoreboard, came back at night, dressed in black, to remove the "DOWN" and "YDS TO GO" signs. They were arrested.

These stories illustrate what I call "The Power of the Clipboard." It basically means that if you look like you know what you are doing, people (even those in positions of authority) will leave you alone.

I have done a lot of trade show work in my career. Most convention facilities have strict (albeit silly) rules on what you can do yourself, and what you must pay their employees to do. The financial penalties for not following these rules can be substantial. Early on, I figured out that if you carry a clipboard, you could do pretty much anything you want with impunity. The clipboard says, "This guy knows what he's doing." Very often I don't even have anything on the clipboard – it is that powerful.

I am not condoning illegal activity. Stu and I knew that Taylor Stadium had a fast-approaching date with a wrecking ball, so we were just trying to preserve some Lehigh history. In the high school scenario, (had anyone asked) what I was doing was completely sanctioned, though they never said a word.

HERE'S THE TAKEAWAY:
BE CONFIDENT IN EVERYTHING YOU DO.

My father-in-law was a successful surgeon, and in telling stories about his four-decades in the OR, he used to say: "sometimes right, sometimes wrong, never in doubt!"

When you are fully committed to your goals and look like you know what you're doing, the world will clear a path for you.

As you go through the days ahead, wipe your mind and heart of any uncertainty. If you want to actually grab a clipboard, go get one, they're not expensive. You will be shocked at how roadblocks will just disappear before you.

4 – NO TRAINING WHEELS ALLOWED!

Growing up in the Nazarian house, there was a predictable schedule for bicycle ownership. As soon as you were able, you could ride the family tricycle. When you were ready, there was a super-small, beater of a two-wheeler that anyone was allowed to try. At age 6, you got your own, brand new two-wheeler. And on your eleventh birthday (or thereabouts) you received your 10-speed.

THERE WERE NO TRAINING WHEELS. YOU LEARNED TO RIDE A TWO-WHEELER BY FALLING OFF, UNTIL YOU DIDN'T.
IT MAY SEEM HARSH, BUT IT WAS RUTHLESSLY EFFECTIVE.

In the summer of 1977 I was eight and a half and I was a child of prodigious curiosity. I have always been fascinated with things mechanical, and bicycles were an early interest to me, mostly because they were accessible.

One afternoon I rode my banana-yellow Schwinn Bantam into the garage and as I looked down to move the kickstand into standing position, my gaze fixed on the coaster brake.

The Schwinn Bantam - The Toyota Camry of 1970s bicycles

In the years since, I have learned that most people simply accept things like the coaster brake. As they learned to ride a bike, kids are told that if they pedal forward the bike will go forward and if they pedal backwards the bike will stop. When they get on a bike, and it behaves as stated, that's the end of the mental exercise. There is little desire to learn more.

As my left foot moved the kickstand from the position horizontal to the vertical, I looked at the coaster brake and I simply couldn't take it any more. I flipped the bike upside down so it was perched on the three-point stance made by the handlebars and the seat. I grabbed the kickstand with my right hand, returning it to its previous out of the way position and I went down to the basement in search of tools.

A few minutes later I emerged with several wrenches, screwdrivers and pliers. I quickly loosened the rear wheel, removed the chain and lay the wheel down on the garage floor. Without any knowledge of what I was doing and not knowing enough to take notes or exercise any form of organization, I went to town, removing every nut, flange, washer, and bolt.

I TOOK THE WHOLE THING APART, EVERYTHING.

As I sat on the garage floor looking at all the parts, I realized that although I now had a pretty good idea how it all worked, I had no clue at all how to put it all back together. I had disassembled the guts of the rear wheel hub so quickly that I had failed to note (mentally or otherwise) how it had all gone together.

It was at this point my Dad walked into the garage and asked what I was doing. I explained that I was figuring out how my coaster brake worked. He looked at the disorganized pile of parts hanging from my greasy hands and said: "well, you better put it back together." He then turned and walked into the laundry room. Remember, this is the house of no training wheels.

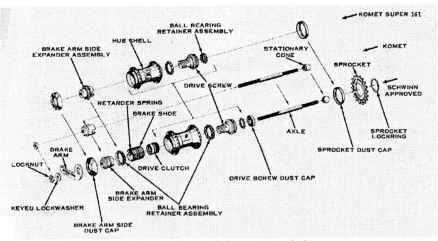

An exploded diagram of a Schwinn coaster brake

After two failed attempts, I thought enough to grab my brother's bike to use as a reference. I was able to separate the inside parts from the outside parts. Little by little, step-by-step I finally succeeded in putting it all back together. As I hopped on the bike for the final test, never before had the simple act of pedaling forward for forward, and backwards to stop held such significance.

I HAD CROSSED THE LINE FROM BLIND ACCEPTANCE, TO INTIMATE KNOWLEDGE – AND IT WAS EXHILARATING.

Since that day I have become increasingly comfortable with taking things apart and putting them back together. Of course the advent of the Internet and the availability of exploded diagrams has made this process easier, but it is still a little daunting every time I take a screwdriver to something new.

The hardest thing I've ever taken apart was our gas-powered, two-stroke leaf blower. The damn pull-string wouldn't go back in. I had a diagram, and by the time it was apart, I had covered our entire four-foot by six-foot kitchen table with parts. I was as shocked as anyone when I put it all back together and it worked.

I don't recommend taking things apart just for curiosity's sake. Most modern things don't have a lot to see inside other than a circuit board. However, if something breaks and you think you can fix it, here are the steps to follow:

1. Google the name of broken thing with the term "exploded diagram"

2. Print out two copies of the diagram, one for notes and one for reference

3. Lay out a white sheet (one you don't mind getting dirty) on a very large surface

4. Take detailed notes (and take pictures with your phone) as you take things apart

5. Make sure you have masking tape, some zipper baggies and a Sharpie to keep things labeled and organized

6. Once you've fixed the broken thing, all you have to do is reverse the process

One of the most common repairs today is that of a broken smartphone or tablet. Most people are terrified to even approach such a thing, but they shouldn't be. There are several companies that sell kits of parts with instruction sheets for the most common phone and tablet repairs.

They are also hundreds of videos out there that show you how to do the just about every repair. Recently the battery on my iPhone wasn't working too well. I ordered a kit for $29, watched the video and when the kit arrived I was able to replace the battery in 15 minutes.

Everyone is more cable of fixing things than they think they are. If it breaks, fix it – I dare you. And if you think you need the help of training wheels, remember to continue to fall until you don't. That approach has always worked in my family.

In the days to come, look for opportunities to get deeper into something than you normally would.

If you have a broken thing lying around, get on the Internet and fix it. Is there a crack in the screen of any smartphone in your house? I bet there is. Order the parts, watch the videos and prepare to be amazed at what you're capable of. Sure, you'll make a few mistakes, but when you succeed, it will feel like that first time you rode a two-wheeler – and I don't know anyone who doesn't want to feel that again.

5 – NO MATTER WHAT, SHOW UP.

Monday January 4, 1993 was the first day of what I consider to be my first real job.

Just about a year before I had moved out of my childhood home in Rochester, NY to New York City to pursue what ended up being a very short lived run at a career in acting/directing/writing. After about four months of going to cattle calls, being turned down by agents and generally no positive indicators at all, I was almost out of money. I answered an ad in the New York Times for an IT consulting firm that was looking for technical writers.

Of course as a recent college graduate, I had no experience as a technical writer. Though I did have an English degree and I had worked in the college computer store for three years. So using the *Transitive Property of Equality* I surmised that:

I KNOW HOW TO WRITE, I KNOW ABOUT COMPUTERS, THEREFORE I CAN WRITE ABOUT COMPUTERS.

Luckily, they agreed and I was hired by the consulting firm to work as a contractor for the software division of Bell Atlantic. It was a pretty good job, and I did it well for about nine months, but it was boring. Furthermore it was an hour commute to Princeton, NJ every day, even after I had moved out of Manhattan to northern New Jersey.

So, in December 1992, I applied for and was offered a job as a technical writer for Crest Audio, Inc. in Paramus, NJ. Now that I had actual experience, getting through the door was much easier.

This was pretty much a dream job for me since I have been an audio nerd my entire life, and now they were going to pay me to play with magic boxes covered in blinky lights, and write about them.

A week before my first day, I slid my two month old 1993 Saturn SL1 across a patch of ice into a curb resulting in damage that required parts be ordered. Since there was New Year's Day and a weekend in the mix, my car would still be in the shop on my first day at the new job, making it fairly difficult for me to get there. My roommate did not have a car and I had no other friends or family near by.

In the years since, I have had the privilege of managing several dozen people in a variety of roles. Believe me when I tell you I have heard the full spectrum of reasons, explanations and excuses as to why someone won't be able to make it to work.

HERE'S THE FUNNY THING...
IT NEVER OCCURRED TO ME TO NOT SHOW UP.

My new job was in Paramus NJ, fourteen miles from my apartment in West New York, New Jersey. No joke, there is a town called West New York, New Jersey.

In the days leading up to my first day, I gathered bus schedules and transit maps. I figured out how taking three different buses across northern NJ, I could get to within a mile of my new office. I decided I would Rollerblade the rest of the way. Given the way the buses ran, I would need to get on the first one by 6:15 am if I was to make it to the office by 9:00. It was going to be a very slow fourteen miles.

The buses ran as expected and I was deposited at my last stop at 8:30, giving me more than enough time to skate the last mile.

Just down the street from the entrance to my new office park is a tricky three-way intersection that was, at the time, managed by a traffic cop during rush hour. As I skated through the intersection on that chilly January morning, the cop sneered at me and said "not in this town, punk!"

Of course I was already through the intersection by the time I processed what he had said, so I simply continued on. I got to work in plenty of time to clean myself up in the bathroom before meeting my new boss promptly at 9:00. She asked why I was carrying Rollerblades, so I explained the situation. She said, "wow, and you managed to get here anyway, huh?" She seemed both baffled and pleased at the same time. Later in the day she offered me a ride home, and I took it.

The next day it was snowing. Rollerblading on the street is dangerous enough, but skating on a wet, cold, potentially icy street is downright foolish. So I decided to ride my bike.

As a regular rider of fifty or more miles at a time, a fourteen-mile jaunt to work seemed like it would be easy. Of course it was 1993, so there was no GPS, Google Maps or anything of the sort. I was stuck with that awful map they used to put in the front of the phone book.

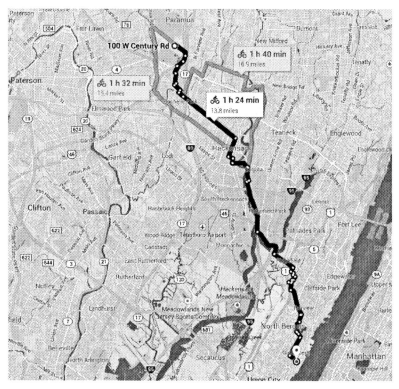

If I'd had Google back then, this would have been my route

I set out at 7:00, figuring even if I got lost I could average seven miles an hour.

I WAS RIGHT... I GOT LOST, AND BADLY.

When I finally found my way to familiar territory it was 8:45. I hit the cop-controlled intersection going about fifteen miles an hour. I was cold, wet and not happy. As I passed the aforementioned law enforcement professional, he barked at me, "not a very nice day for a bike ride is it?" I rode the last block and thought to myself that he might well be the most unpleasant person I'd ever encountered.

I got to work on time and was able to clean myself up and stash my bike down by the loading dock. That night I rode home without incident; it took me fifty minutes. Before I set out for home, I called the repair shop and they told me my car would be done the next afternoon.

That last morning I was able to ride to work in forty-five minutes. As I approached my traffic cop friend I was ready. If he said something, I was going to have some kind of clever retort that would send his feeble mind reeling. I approached him intentionally slower than I had the day before, but he just waved me through and said nothing. As I coasted into my office park I thought to myself, "well played copper, well played."

Later that afternoon a coworker gave me a ride to the station where I was able to catch a train to my car. I left my bike at the office and picked it up the next day. I worked at Crest Audio for almost five years and never had to take alternate transportation again.

Benjamin Disraeli, the British Conservative politician, writer and aristocrat who twice served as Prime Minister once said,

"HISTORY IS WRITTEN BY THOSE WHO SHOW UP."

I can't say how true that is, but what I can tell you, is that someone who honors their obligations and respects the people and organizations to whom they have made commitments, is already far ahead of those who don't. Better to inconvenience yourself then to call and explain why a problem you are experiencing is now someone else's too.

Our society has become entirely too comfortable with explaining "why not," and lost the drive to just make things happen.

If someone is expecting you – show up. No matter what you have to go through to be there, you'll be glad you did.

Think about the commitments you make, especially in relation to your intent to keep them. If someone invites out with a group for drinks, don't say, "I'll try and get there" if you have no plans to do so.

If you make a time commitment of any kind, deliver it early. And here's the best one: try and be early to every appointment and meeting you have this week. If a meeting starts late, you won't be the cause, and that is a good feeling the just might rub off on others.

6 – BACKGROUND NOISE

In the 1990 movie, *The Hunt For Red October*, there is a scene where a clever sonar operator named Jones, finds something in a sound where nobody else could.

The Americans are trolling around the North Atlantic looking for a Soviet sub called the *Red October*. This particular sub had a new mode of propulsion making it effectively invisible to conventional sonar by blending in with the ambient noises of the ocean.

So after listening to hours and hours of what everyone thought were simply normal sounds, the sonar operator decides to try something. He takes a recording of the "nothing" and speeds it up. When he does this he hears a mechanical clicking noise that does not sound like the ocean.

In discussing what he has found, the dialogue between him and Commander Mancuso goes like this:

Jones: When I asked the computer to identify it, what I got was 'magma displacement.' You see, sir, SAPS software was originally written to look for seismic events. And when it gets confused, it kind of 'runs home to mama.'
Mancuso: I'm not following you, Jonesy.
Jones: Sorry, sir. Listen to it at times speed. [Plays tape.] Now that's gotta be man made, Captain.
Mancuso: Have I got this straight, Jonesy? A forty million dollar computer tells you you're chasing an earthquake, but you don't believe it? And you come up with this on your own?
Jones: Yes, sir.
Mancuso: Including all the navigational math?
Jones: Sir, I-I've got-
Mancuso: Relax, Jonesy, you sold me!
The Soviet sub could sonically disappear, but Jonsey figured a way to flush them out – he filtered out the background noise.

New Years Day 2006 was cold and sunny. My wife Emily had risen early to go into the hospital to be the pediatrician-on-call in the intensive care unit for the day, leaving me alone with the four children: Charlotte 5, Lewis 4, Oliver 3, and my youngest Lawrence was two weeks shy of his second birthday.

We slept a little later than normal, but after breakfast it quickly became clear that we needed to get out of the house. Since it was winter in Rochester we opted for the best thing one can ever do on such a day: go sledding.

My high school "go-to" hill in Ellison Park was more than my diminutive kids could handle, so I opted for a slightly smaller hill in Mendon Ponds Park. After all, this was going to be Lawrence's first sledding experience; I needed to start him off slowly, but not too slowly.

I installed fresh diapers for those who needed them, and bundled everyone up in their snuggly best. We loaded two plastic sleds into the back of the Grand Caravan and off we went.

Being the morning of New Year's Day, the park was empty. We unloaded, and quickly covered the short walk to the top of the hill.

The sledding hill at Mendon Ponds Park – that day we had it to ourselves

The sunshine reflecting off the bright, white snow was almost unbearable, but when you live in a place that must endure a long, dark winter you'll put up with just about anything for a sunny day, even partial blindness.

Charlotte and Lewis were old pros, making quick work of sledding down and jaunting back up the hill. Oliver did a couple runs, but ultimately decided the thrill of the sled was not worth the effort of the walk. Since I refused to carry him back up, he plunked himself down at the top of the hill content to just watch.

Lawrence seemed to be enjoying his first day on the hill. He and I shared a few runs together, but not too long into the fun, Charlotte and Lewis were begging to have a go with their youngest brother.

I loaded all three of them into a single sled, Charlotte at the bow, Lawrence in the middle and Lewis manning the stern. By this time they had worn some nice, slick trails into the hill. We maneuvered the sled to the top of one of the trails and let it fly.

They got off to a good start, but Lawrence's boots were hanging off the side of the sled, not such that they were slowing them down, but enough that a steady stream of snow was being kicked up into his face. The three of them were actually going pretty fast.

I WATCHED POWERLESS FROM THE TOP OF THE HILL, NEXT TO OLIVER WHO WAS VOLUNTARILY STUFFING HIS FACE WITH SNOW.

Lawrence started screaming, and as they reached the bottom of the hill the sled did one of those ninety-degree fishtails and tipped over on its right side as it came to rest.

With one eye on a stationary Oliver, I sprinted down the hill to quell the crying and make everyone happy again. By the time I got to them, Lawrence was in a full-blown howl. Charlotte and Lewis were dusting themselves off, but seemed no worse for the experience.

I brushed the snow from Lawrence's rosy face, but that didn't help, and he continued to cry as I carried him back up the hill. We both sat down with Oliver while Charlotte and Lewis continued to sled for the next thirty minutes.

Lawrence calmed down, and not too much later we decided to call it a day. As I carried him back to the car he whined a little, but generally he seemed better. When we got back to the van, I put the sleds in back, but as I was loading Lawrence into his car seat he started screaming again. I figured he had a loaded diaper, so I simply slid the door closed and decided I would change it at home. As we drove the twenty minutes home, the kids were fairly quiet in their seats.

We pulled into the driveway and as I pulled Lawrence from his car seat, he started crying again. "Okay buddy, I'll change your diaper now and you'll be happy," I said as we walked into the house.

Without putting him down I pulled my youngest out of his snowsuit, but his reaction was ugly. As I tugged the zipper past his waist, Lawrence started crying again.

> **I THOUGHT TO MYSELF**
> **THAT THIS MUST BE ONE WHOPPER OF A DIAPER LOAD.**

I carried the screaming child across the kitchen and to the changing station in the family room. I laid him down expecting the mother of all doodies, but as I cracked open the Huggie; I saw nothing. To say the least I was confused, so I began a little investigation.

After a few minutes of poking and prodding I found the problem, the boy had a broken leg.

My Brother Doug's wife is also an intensive care physician, and he and I have always joked that when our wives leave us home on the weekend with the children, our only job is to keep them out of the emergency room. As we drove to the hospital, I called my brother to inform him that I was the first one to fall. To this day, he still has a perfect record.

Now I recognize that "father of the year" is not exactly the right term to describe a guy who managed to miss a broken leg on his two-year-old for the better part of an hour, but in my defense I give you two words: background noise.

At the time, Lawrence's modes of communicating were as follows:

- I'm hungry = Cry
- I have a load in my pants = Cry
- I have soap in my eyes = Cry
- I'm tired = Cry
- My brother/sister just stole my toy = Cry
- The dog just stole my cookie = Cry
- I just got snow in my face from sledding too fast = Cry

SO, HOW WAS I TO KNOW THIS PARTICULAR CRY WAS A NEW ONE – BROKEN LEG?

The world we live in is noisy. We are so accustomed to a minimum of background noise that we don't even remember what quiet is until the occasional power outage.

Take some time to look at the nosiest parts of your life, and try to develop some filters to help you see and hear things, despite what is omnipresent in the background. If you can manage it, you might find a missing submarine, the reason your baby is crying, and maybe, just maybe, something else entirely.

Whenever I feel overwhelmed by all the noise around me, I put on some music, but instead of taking it all in, I focus on a single instrument.

If I am listening to pop or rock music, I like to zero in on the bass guitar. For classical, I try and pick out something more obscure like the Oboe, the English horn or the French horn.

You'll be surprised how doing this for just one song will sharpen your ability to filter out other things in your life.

It might allow you to better hear your spouse in the presence of screaming kids. It could help you hear the subtleties of what a coworker is saying. It can also help you eavesdrop on conversations at your local coffee shop – which can be fascinating.

Every day this week pick at least one song, one you think you know well, and focus on that single instrument. You will come to realize that you didn't know that song as well as you thought you did.

Now try that everywhere!

Stephen S. Nazarian

7 – ONE WAY TO DISARM A BULLY

In the summer of 1984, I was part of a local trip of forty boy scouts to the Philmont National Scout Ranch in New Mexico The trip had three legs:

1. A two-week bus trip out to New Mexico, via a long list of interesting stops

2. Twelve days at Philmont, made up of a ten day, 120 mile hike plus a day at base camp on either side

3. A two-day breakneck bus ride home

Each group of ten boys was called a "crew" and the hike we were headed for was called a "trek." Every crew had ten scouts, a volunteer adult leader, and an elected boy leader. There were months of preparatory meetings, and training hikes. It was at the end of these "shakedown" exercises that each crew elected their boy leader. In the case of my crew, they elected me.

The trip left from a parking lot in downtown Rochester, at 9:30pm and we drove through the night, and all the next day before reaching our first destination.

For those of you who've never met me personally – I'm a bit of a talker. At age fifteen, it was worse than it is now. That is to say, I was a kid who wouldn't shut the hell up.

Making matters worse I was pretty much a nerd. I tended to talk about nerdy things like school while never talking about cooler things like sports.

FORTUNATELY, ON A BUS WITH FORTY BOY SCOUTS, THERE WERE PLENTY OF OTHER NERDS WITH WHOM I COULD CHAT.

However, there were a few "cool" kids on the bus, and within the early hours of that first night on the bus I managed to catch the attention of, and annoy, the bulliest of them.

I do not remember his name so let's call him Tom. He was short, maybe 5' 3" with blazing red hair.

I remember being in the middle of an enthusiastic exchange with one of my new friends; we were having a debate about earth science (yeah I know, ok). I was turned around in my bus seat, looking over the headrest at the other kid, and if my memory serves me correctly we were discussing glacial formations like drumlins, eskers and kettles. Again – I know.

I was in the middle of what was most likely a well formed, but completely nerdy argument, when Tom punched me in the arm and said, "shut up dweeb, we don't want to hear about your nerd shit."

AND SO IT BEGAN. TOM WAS THE BULLY AND I WAS TO BE THE OBJECT OF HIS BULLY BEHAVIOR.

This was nothing new to me. I was never consistently bullied for years and years like you hear about today, and I thank God that I grew up before the Internet and social media. I had however been the focus of more than one person looking to pump himself up by beating me down. I was a tall, skinny, smart, not-too-cool, kid who had no sports skills – textbook bully bait.

Throughout the two-week trip out, we stopped at famous places like Yellowstone and Grand Teton national parks, as well as some lesser known places like The Corn Palace and Wall Drug. At every stop Tom did his best to get in my face, play pranks on me and do whatever he could to make me look the fool in front of his little group of bully disciples. Most of my friends were simply content to be invisible to Tom, since I think many of them were happy to be away from bullies at home.

MY GOAL EVERY DAY WAS SIMPLY TO AVOID HIM.

After two weeks, we finally got to Philmont and since Tom was in a different crew, I wouldn't be encountering him at all for the next ten days. Philmont is 137,500 acres, that's a lot of wilderness in which to get lost.

As it turned out, Tom was the elected boy leader of his crew. When we got to base camp, the boy leaders had a lot of responsibilities as we prepared to head out on the trail. At one point we all had to stand in a long line (maybe 100 or more of us) to pick up packets of information for our respective crews. I had showed up early and had a place in line near the front. It was hot, and the New Mexican sun was as intense as the line was slow.

I looked back, and about sixty boys behind me, close to the end of the line, was Tom. His height made him hard to see sometimes, but once you caught a glimpse of his hair he was hard to miss.

As I looked in his direction, our eyes met and without thinking I did something crazy; I motioned for him to come over to me. At first he thought I was talking to someone else, but after my repeated hand motions he knew I was talking to him. He gave me a look that I can only describe as the one made about a 1,000 times by Ben Stiller's character in *Dodgeball*.

After a moment, he strutted over to me and incredulously grunted, "WHAT?" I replied, "I thought you might want to move up to my place in line."

HE WAS SPEECHLESS. HE STOOD SILENTLY NEXT TO ME IN LINE FOR A FEW MINUTES AND THEN SIMPLY SAID, "THANKS MAN."

For the remainder of the trip I had no trouble at all with Tom, and in fact on the bus trip home he was overtly nice to me more than once.

The experience of time has given me an understanding of what my gut told me to do those three decades ago. I took away the bully's only weapon, fear. By calling him towards me I showed him that I wasn't afraid. Then, offering kindness to someone who had shown me nothing but vitriol and malice completely disarmed him.

I'm not saying that all bully situations are this simple. I know that the majority of them are more complex. However, the lesson I learned that day has served me well every day since.

YOU DON'T ALWAYS HAVE TO PLAY THE GAME BEING PRESENTED TO YOU.

Sometimes changing the rules will give you the advantage you need to succeed. Tom had decided that he was going to be the bully and I was to be his victim. Initially I accepted my role, but through my actions I told him, despite how he had treated me, I would prefer to be his friend, or at the very least I refused to accept the role he had assigned me.

Look around your life. Do you have any situations or relationships that aren't heading in the right direction? Think about how you might change the rules.

We all have bullies in our lives. Think about the ones with which you must deal most often. Think about the interactions you have and your standard responses. Now change everything.

For each of the things you do regularly to deal with, avoid and manage this person – figure out what the opposite is. It will feel very strange, but start using these opposite approaches.

It might work immediately or it might take a while, or it may never have a meaningful effect. However, I can promise you this; a bully will never see it coming and at minimum you will enjoy watching him (or her) try and figure out just what the hell you're up to. At the very least you will have changed the game and that is a step in the right direction.

8 – HOT DOG DEATH ROW

Thomas Edison was once asked how he felt about his failures, he answered: "I have not failed 10,000 times. I have not failed once. I have succeeded in proving that those 10,000 ways will not work. When I have eliminated the ways that will not work, I will find the way that will work."

This is in line with what Albert Einstein said about ideas, "For an idea that does not first seem insane, there is no hope."

It is with these two pieces of advice, from two of the greatest minds in human history, that I bring you the story of the ten-year-old and the **Hot Dog Cooker**.

When I was ten years old, I used to ride my yellow Schwinn two-wheeler to the Penfield Public Library. This was back when the Library was in the rickety old town hall building in the village center. Science books were my thing, especially anything that included projects I could build at home with household products and scraps of stuff.

One day I happened onto a book called ***Safe Electrical Experiments for Children***. Clearly, this had everything I was looking for. There were experiments, they were safe, and since I was a child, they were designed with me in mind. It never occurred to me that I should talk to any grownups before heading out to the garage to get busy.

After flipping through the pages, I decided to start with something that looked both fun and practical – **The Electric Hot Dog Cooker**. The device looked fairly straightforward and required the following short list of parts:

- 1 Piece of ¾" scrap wood at least 6" x 8"
- 4 Glass baby food jars
- 2 #12 common nails
- 1 110 volt lamp cord with a plug on the end
- 1 Hot dog

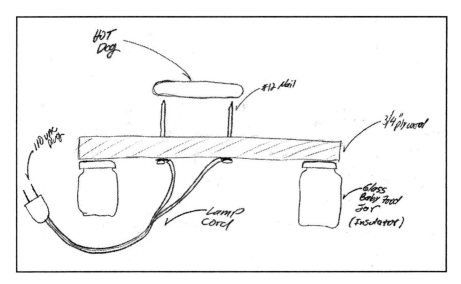

My best recollection of the diagram from the book

I have scoured the Internet for a copy of this book, but it seems to have been wiped off the face of the earth, and for good reason. If the other "experiments" in this book were as safe as the one I describe here, it was a substantial danger to children everywhere. That said, I was a kid, it was the 1980s and I was determined to build this practical kitchen gadget.

Of course I did not have EXACTLY what the list called for, but I did my best. I had the wood, the nails, the lamp cord and I knew we had hot dogs. Since my younger sister was already eight, we didn't have any baby food jars in the house, but we had other glass jars, but not four the same size. The glass was supposed to serve as an insulator so you might reduce the chance of electrocuting yourself, while preparing your nitrate-filled snack, but four different ones sort of defeated this part of the plan. I taped scraps of wood to the bottoms of the shorter jars to make it level, sort of.

I gathered all the parts and was sitting on the garage floor assembling them together when my neighbor Mr. Nussbaum walked by. He saw me working away and poked his head into the garage to see what I was up to. I explained my plan, showed him the book and my progress thus far. He smiled, nodded and then turned to walk home.

I GUESS HE WAS HORRIFIED BY WHAT I WAS DOING, BECAUSE HE IMMEDIATELY CALLED MY MOTHER AND ENCOURAGED HER TO COME OUT TO THE GARAGE AND GET 'INVOLVED' IN MY PROJECT.

Not wanting to quash my budding engineering enthusiasm, my mother came out and asked what I was making, so I innocently explained. I think she was sufficiently taken aback by my plan, but she calmly encouraged me to finish, but insisted that I NOT plug it in until my father got home. I agreed.

I completed the medieval looking contraption and waited for my Dad to get home. I waited – and waited.

When my Dad finally got home, I thought I might explode I was so excited. I was convinced that I had created the next kitchen counter convenience sensation. After being briefed by my mom, Dad brought the device into the kitchen for what would undoubtedly be the first of many tasty hot dog preparations.

THE CONDEMNED WIENER WAS PLACED ON THE NAILS, ALL FAMILY MEMBERS WERE ASKED TO STEP BACK SEVERAL FEET, AND THEN MY DAD PLUGGED IT IN.

What happened next wasn't pretty. Remember that scene in *The Green Mile* with the botched electrocution? Well that was pretty much what we saw, but at least it was only a hot dog. My son Lawrence (who was ten when we did this) and I recreated the ill-fated device, which you can see below. However, it turns out that the quality of hot dogs has improved over the years because in the latest build the hot dog just, well, cooked.

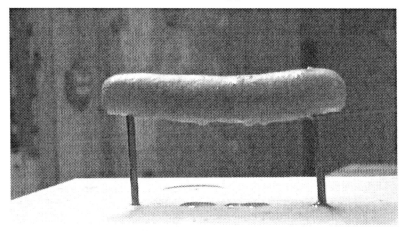

The 2014 recreation of the Hot Dog Cooker

All other things considered the device did perform as advertised. The hot dog did in fact get hot. Unfortunately, the taste of an electrocuted hot dog is, in a word, nasty.

In isolation, this story looks like the tale of a goofy kid who got his hands on an ill-conceived book and managed not to hurt himself. But, if you look a little deeper, you'll see that it is really about the value in the exercise of the absurd.

As children, it seems normal to try anything because we don't know better. It is these consequence-free flights of fancy that lead to greater, deeper and wider discovery. Sometimes, if we don't embrace the strange place, we'll never get beyond it.

So, the next time something seems too silly to consider, stop being a grown-up for a minute and just get in there; build a Hot Dog Cooker. However, watch out for Mr. Nussbaum, he'll blow you in as soon as look at you.

How often do you not share an idea for fear it might be considered crazy or stupid? Do your kids every come to you with wacky ideas that you dismiss or discourage because they sound messy or (even worse) dangerous?

For the next week, resist the urge to quash crazy ideas, no matter the source. In fact I dare you to embrace them and enthusiastically see them through.

Most of them will be colossal failures, but maybe, just maybe one will work. At the very least you will learn a lot and have a ton of fun trying.

For every success, there are enumerable failures. Until you start failing, you'll never see the success you're after.

9 – GOOD BOYS DON'T LOOK IN THE BAG

In the winter of 1987 I needed a job. I was in the middle of a loaded high school senior year that included: being the student representative to the school board, editor of the yearbook, captain of the indoor track team plus a full schedule that included some AP courses. I did not have a lot of free time for employment.

Some of my friends had done well delivering pizza, and with my brother away at college and my sister not yet licensed, I had regular access to one of the three family cars. So, in February 1987, I secured a delivery job for a local pizzeria.

Our town had no shortage of pizza places, but this was the newest and while most of the others had many locations, this place was all by itself. The joint was owned by two brothers, both of whom had other jobs, so they were not around much.

THE MENU WAS COMPRISED OF PIZZA, SUBS AND CHICKEN WINGS. IT ALL SEEMED PRETTY NORMAL.

Up to this point in my young life I had worked at a golf course, Burger King, an athletic shoe store, and in the kitchen at a local restaurant. For each of these jobs, I had filled out some paperwork and when payday came, I was given a check that represented my hours multiplied by the minimum wage, minus taxes; normal right?

THE FINANCIAL ARRANGEMENT AT THE PIZZERIA SHOULD HAVE BEEN MY FIRST CLUE THAT THIS PLACE WAS NOT ON THE LEVEL.

The deal was: $1 an hour, plus $1 a delivery, plus tips. We were paid every Friday, in cash, via an envelope marked only with our initials in pencil. The whole thing was sketchy to say the least.

Fortunately, the seemingly illegal pay arrangement ended up being a pretty good deal. On a weekend night I would come home with $50-$60 cash for about seven hours work. After I paid for gas, that was around $7 an hour – more than twice the minimum wage of $3.35, and tax free.

YOU LIVED AND DIED BY YOUR TIPS.

An average night looked like this: you'd make $7 for putting in the time and maybe another $15 for the deliveries you did. The rest came from tips, and I found out early on that creativity was the key. One guy used to do his deliveries wearing a tuxedo. He looked very nice but I have no idea if that improved his tips.

After paying close attention to what made a good and bad tipper, I came to the conclusion that when harried parents and kids were involved, the tip was either small or didn't happen at all.

So, one day I drove downtown to a magic shop and purchased a gross of "wiener dog balloons." I quickly taught myself how to make balloon animals (we had no YouTube for such things) and every time a customer came to the door with a kid, I pulled out a balloon and made a little doggie.

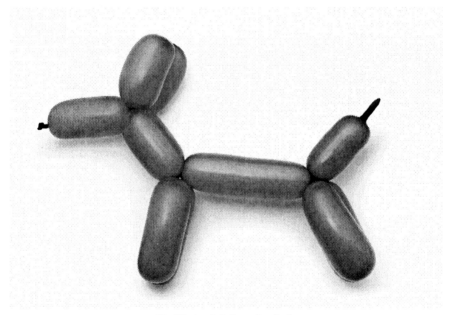

The little doggie that saved my tips!

My tip average went from $0.85 to $3.00 per delivery.

The balloon did two things: it made the kid happy, and it gave the parent the extra thirty seconds they needed to remember to tip the pizza guy. I mean, who wouldn't tip a guy who was making their kid happy, right?

I SHOULD HAVE STUCK WITH PIZZA DELIVERY.

As the school year ended, the brothers asked if I would be interested in managing the joint for the summer. I would be paid $6 an hour and either work eleven to eight, or four to midnight, pretty much every day. If I stayed on the job for the whole summer, they would pay me an extra $1 an hour, retroactive bonus before I went to college in August.

At eighteen years old, I was not familiar with the term "retention bonus" but for a pizza joint to offer me one should have been a red flag. The entire deal was verbal, but I agreed to it anyway.

Most of the time things were okay, and I got to eat all the pizza, subs and wings I wanted. However, as I was exposed to more and more of the "business operations," it became clear to me that something was just not right.

Some of my suspicions came simply from how the owners behaved. Everything was done in cash; I mean everything. There were two specific events however that made me very uncomfortable.

As the weather got warmer, the brothers decided that pizza, subs, and wings weren't enough. They wanted to sell ice cream. A local creamery offered to lend them a display freezer as part of a deal to sell their ice cream. So, one day I came in to work and in the middle of the already cramped space was this giant ice cream freezer.

THE PIZZERIA WAS ALREADY HOT, BUT ADDING A GIANT ICE CREAM FREEZER MADE IT EVEN HOTTER.

A couple of months into the ice cream run, a salesman for a regional ice cream supplier stopped in. He promised to sell ice cream to the brothers for half what they were paying the local place. They of course made the deal and started loading up the freezer with the cheaper product. They were also stupid enough to hang the three-foot plastic ice cream cone bearing the name of the new supplier from the awning in front of the building.

It didn't take long for the salesman from the local creamery to drive by and notice the logo of his competitor prominently hanging from our awning. He came storming in, saw the other ice cream in his freezer and went ballistic.

It just so happened that the brothers were there at the time, and the situation quickly descended into a tornado of f-bombs and threats. The salesman left screaming.

It was clear to me that my employers were 100% in the wrong, yet after the salesman peeled away in his car; the brothers went on for at least half an hour with a litany of profanity about how they had been cheated and screwed.

IT WAS OFFICIAL... I WAS WORKING FOR CRAZY PEOPLE.

The next day when I arrived to set up for lunch I was told that the "rat-bastards" from the local creamery were coming for their freezer and I was NOT to let them take it. Keep in mind I was eighteen years old, 6' 2" and I weighed-in at maybe 145 lbs.

"PENCIL-NECKED GEEK" WAS AN APT DESCRIPTION OF MY PHYSICAL FORM.

Around 2:00pm, a small flatbed truck pulled up to the front door. Two guys each about twice my size walked sideways through the door and said they were there for the freezer. I let them take it.

Of course I had to scramble to squeeze all the ice cream into the other freezers we had, but I managed to make it work. That was the end of the brothers' ice cream venture.

The other event that puzzles me to this day went down like this.

I came in around 4:00pm to run the place until closing at midnight. As one of the brothers was leaving, he turned to me and said, "hey Steve, there's a guy coming in later. His name is Tony. There's a white bag in the walk-in cooler for him. Don't look in it." He then turned back towards the door and left.

SERIOUSLY, DID THAT JUST HAPPEN?

I opened the door to the walk-in to make sure that the bag was actually there; it was. The bag was white paper, like the one you'd get from a bakery. It was large, but not as big as a grocery bag. I closed the cooler door and tried to ignore the situation.

Around 7:00pm, a white Lincoln Continental pulled up to the front door and a 5' 2" "Tony" hopped out. In a shiny suit, black shirt and white tie, he swaggered into the joint like Joe Pesci in a scene from *Goodfellas*. He walked to the counter, looked up at me and said "I'm Tony, you got sump'n for me?

I said that I did, and calmly walked into the cooler for the bag. I carefully brought it out and placed it on the counter in front of him. It weighed maybe three pounds. He leaned in and still looking up at me said, "did jew look in it?" I politely replied, "um, no."

In one smooth motion, he grabbed the bag with his left hand and slapped me on the cheek with his right saying "good boy;" the stare of his beady little eyes never losing contact with mine. He and the bag hopped back into the Lincoln and they drove off.

THE TRANSACTION WAS NEVER MENTIONED AGAIN.

Of course as the summer came to a close and I was getting ready to go to college, I asked about the bonus that was promised to me. The brothers said I must have misunderstood. What they meant was that if I stayed the summer and didn't end up going to college that they would give me a raise.

YES, I'M SURE I MISUNDERSTOOD, SILLY ME.

There is a southern expression that goes like this: "Don't piss down my neck and tell me it's raining."

I left that pizzeria soaked and smelly.

Over the years I have learned a lot of lessons about vetting employers before signing up for a particular job, but I will say that I have yet to learn as much on the subject in such a short time as I did in the summer of 1987.

I will never know exactly what was going on in that pizzeria, but I can tell you this: if an employment situation doesn't feel right, walk away. Your gut has no reason to lie to you.

Do you listen to your gut, or do you ignore it like an annoying coworker or classmate? For the next week, ignore all the rational data and go with your gut every time is speaks up.

Think of your gut as a decision engine that has all the data from your entire life. It does not provide rationale or an argument, but rather it leads you like an experienced dancer.

You may end up doing things that others might consider wrong or reckless, but remember that your gut only flourishes if you do, so listen to it. It only wants what's best for both of you.

Stephen S. Nazarian

10 – THE HOOK

In 1994, the band Blues Traveler released an album called *Four*. On that album was a song called *Hook* and if you know the song at all, you probably know it all too well. It certainly qualifies for the designation of an *Ear Worm*, and by that I mean a song that simply sticks with you – good or bad.

There has been a lot of chatter in recent years about "personal branding" and I'm still not sure what I think about the idea. However, I can tell you that a "hook" is something we can all use to further our goals, both business and personal.

One spring, my family was on vacation in Virginia Beach, and we attended Easter Sunday services at a church just off the boardwalk with other local family members. After the service, I was talking to my brother-in-law about the sermon and he said, "Yeah, the priest always opens and closes his sermons with a joke. They are usually a little funnier than today's were though."

In a similar vein, our church at home received a new priest several months ago, and one of the first things he did was tell the congregation that when he says "hi" we should all respond with "hello," and conversely when he says "hello" we should all say "hi." After about three weeks we were all doing it.

I don't know if this is part of the curriculum they are teaching these days in seminary, but these two priests have a "hook." The 8th and 9th definitions of the word according to merriam-webster.com are:

- A device especially in music or writing that catches the attention
- A selling point or marketing scheme

Hooks are something I have used in the past, and I will continue to use as the situation calls for it.

═══════════════════════════

In 2009, I made a decision to give politics a try. In my hometown of Penfield, NY there was an open seat for Town Supervisor (essentially mayor), and after encouragement from some trusted friends I made a commitment to run.

As the race came together, I found myself running as an independent, against a well known Republican and an upstart Democrat. I did not have the financial resources of my opponents, so at every turn my team and I worked hard to come up with ideas that could raise my profile for little or no cash.

Me and the red tie that became my hook

Our first public event was marching in the Fourth-of-July parade. My supporters were wearing campaign t-shirts and I was dressed in khaki pants, a white dress shirt and a red tie.

As we walked, I shook hands and waved to the gathered crowd while my team of supporters handed out sports water bottles. As they interacted with the crowd, I witnessed several of them pointing in my direction while saying "he's right over there, the guy in the white shirt and red tie."

Without even trying, I had my hook. Throughout the four months of the campaign I always wore a white shirt with a red tie. No matter where I was (grocery store, Starbucks, a kid's soccer game, or going door-to-door) I was easy to pick out. I was the guy in the white shirt and red tie. In the end I garnered only 15% of the vote, but it was an incredible experience and it galvanized my understanding in the power of the hook.

Throughout my professional life I have had the pleasure of speaking to audiences of all sizes. As effective and thrilling as addressing a crowd can be, the best part of such an experience comes in the face-to-face conversations that follow. Usually these speaking engagements are part of a much larger event like a tradeshow or professional conference, and it is often hard for audience members to find the guy who was just on stage (me) in the large crowd of the convention hall.

I MAKE THIS EASIER ON MY AUDIENCE BY EMPLOYING A SHORT-TERM VERSION OF THE HOOK.

When going on stage I make sure I am wearing some very distinctive piece of clothing. I have used a pink bow tie, a loud plaid jacket and a pair of orange glasses (though never all together).

Me in the loud plaid jacket

The point is that people who want to talk to you will approach you in a crowd, but only if they are sure that you are the person they just saw on stage. Without the temporary hook of the "slightly garish" piece of clothing or accessory, they might not be certain and therefore they might not say anything. By being the only six-foot-two brown haired guy in the crowd wearing orange glasses (see back cover), I eliminate that doubt and the conversations can proceed, as they should.

I take issue with Webster's use of the word "scheme" in the definition above because it suggests something unseemly or dishonest, but I assure you – proper use of the hook is both honest and practical.

The heart of effective communication is the complete understanding of human nature and your audience. After all, you can't effectively say what you have to say until you have their attention.

Think about the hook. Use it where you can. I think you'll find that it is a tool as effective as it is fun to use. Blues Traveler nailed it:

Because the Hook brings you back
I ain't tellin' you no lie
The Hook brings you back
On that you can rely

Do you have a hook? If you don't, you probably have something that is "your thing" that you could easily develop into one.

I knew a lady once who always wrapped gifts in the same peacock blue paper. No matter where she and her family went, her gifts stood out. It wasn't a big thing, but it was her thing.

Find the thing that is your thing and don't hide it - celebrate it, grow it, flaunt it.

If you're not sure what your thing should be, ask a few close friends, family members or coworkers, they'll tell you.

11 – LET REST FOR SEVERAL DECADES

There is a meat cooking technique I learned years ago. It turns out that when you take meat off the heat source on which you are cooking it, the cooking doesn't stop.

For the next several minutes, the heat you've been applying continues to affect said piece-o-protein. Then, once that process is complete, over the following few minutes, all kinds of craziness takes place where juices move around and, in the words of Emeril Lagasse, "get all happy."

This is why many recipes that involve meat tell you let the dish "rest" after cooking. Do not skip this step, it is critically important. I once made a rib recipe that called for putting the racks in a double layer, closed paper grocery bag for 30 minutes after they came out of the oven. I thought for sure the ribs would be cold – they were delicious.

═══════════════════════

My father, Lawrence, was born in May 1940, he was the first born of Samuel and Winifred Nazarian. Four years later, his brother Barry was born. My grandfather worked several jobs to support his young family including: running a gas station, driving a soda truck and working in an airplane factory supporting the war effort. At times he worked two or more of these jobs at the same time. My grandmother was a talented artist, but with no formal training she was functionally a homemaker.

My father was thirteen and my uncle was nine when my grandfather, without warning, died of a massive heart attack. He had been a smoker, yes, but working three jobs to support your family has a way of unspooling a life faster than it is supposed to go.

SO, THERE WAS MY GRANDMOTHER WITH TWO BOYS, NO HUSBAND AND NO JOB IN 1953.

In the aftermath of Sam's passing there was help from church, friends and other charities. But after assessing the details of her situation, it became clear that Winifred was going to have to find a job.

At that time, with functional computers still at least forty years away, there were many more jobs for artists than there are today. However, with no formal training my grandmother faced an uphill battle looking for that kind of work. That said she had little choice since she had no other marketable skills. Furthermore, she knew that she was going to have to work long hours to make ends meet, so she wanted to make sure to find a job doing something she loved.

After doing a little research on the minimum amount of education she might need to even apply for a job, she walked through the door of an art school right in her hometown of Montclair New Jersey. She was only interested in finding out how much time and money would be required to earn a certificate that would allow her to start her job search.

OF COURSE TIME AND MONEY WERE TWO THINGS SHE REALLY DIDN'T HAVE, BUT SHE HAD TO START SOMEWHERE.

She stood against the wall by the door; watching the woman who owned the art school, teach a class. My grandmother looked around at all the art on the walls and knew that she could already do as well, if not better work than the pieces she saw hanging.

When the class ended, the teacher came over and introduced herself. Her name was Suzanne. Winifred briefly explained her situation and inquired about the cost and timing of the certificate in which she was interested. Suzanne listened intently and with kind eyes said, "gather up what supplies you have and be here tomorrow morning at nine, we can worry about the tuition once you get your first job as an artist."

It only took a few weeks for my grandmother to earn the certificate she needed, and not long after she was able to begin work as an artist, taking the bus into Manhattan every morning.

Because of the long hours she was working, and the boys she was raising, it was a couple of months before she was able to get back to the art school to settle her debt. One Saturday morning she finally had a little time when she knew the school would be open so, checkbook in hand, she marched up the street to pay the woman who had been so kind to her. When she got to the door, she found it locked and after asking around she learned that the school had closed a few weeks earlier with no forwarding information.

The 1959 Winnie The Pooh game by Parker Brothers - Artwork by my Grandma

Winifred enjoyed a successful and varied career as an artist. She worked at Gimbels department store doing calligraphy for wedding invitations. She worked as an illustrator for the American Book Company, doing illustrations for grade school textbooks. She did work for Parker Brothers, including the box and board for the 1959 *Winnie The Pooh Game.*

Look closely, you'll see it

Since it was the 1950s, and since she was a woman, everything she did was a "work for hire." This meant she never received any credit for her work beyond a paycheck, but we Nazarians are a clever bunch, and know how to get around such things.

Growing up, anything we would get from my grandmother was beautifully adorned with her talent. Even the addressing of the envelopes was pretty enough to frame. In her later years she did a great deal of watercolor painting. She used to say that most of it was "crap", but fortunately she kept every one of them, so now all of her grandchildren have her "crap" framed and hanging in their homes.

One of Winifred Nazarian's "pieces of crap" in my dining room – awful isn't it?

When Winifred was seventy-five, she was visiting a friend in a nursing home, and it occurred to her that she might enjoy visiting with other residents in the home. She inquired about doing such a thing, and she was told to do so, she would need to become a certified nursing assistant. The next day she signed up for a class at the Red Cross, and got certified.

For many years, she walked more than a mile from her apartment, to the nursing home, where she would sit and talk with the residents, just keeping them company. My grandmother was a ruthless Scrabble player, and over the years of vanquishing nearly every opponent she faced, she earned the nickname *One-Eye-Fred*. Only a few of the residents were able to play Scrabble with her. The rest really just wanted someone to sit with and maybe have a chat.

Nursing home residents come and go with high frequency, and my grandmother made many friends who left this life almost as quickly as they had come into her's.

Every day she came to the home, she met with a coordinator who managed her time there. One day she was taken to a new resident whose family was no longer able to care for her – she was suffering from dementia. On her first day she was effectively all-alone in the nursing home. This resident had no sense of her surroundings, but seemed happy enough in her own little world. The coordinator brought my grandmother into the room and said "Winnie, I'd like you to meet Suzanne."

My grandmother had only to look into her kind eyes to know exactly who this woman was. Winnie sat down and said "hello."

Suzanne only lived a few months in the nursing home before passing away, but she was never alone. Every day she possibly could, my grandmother made the uphill walk to the home to sit with Suzanne, even when there was six inches of snow on the ground.

Winifred had always held onto a little hollow feeling inside about not being able to pay the debt she felt she owed to the kind owner of the art school. But the day she met Suzanne in the nursing home, she knew that God had always had different payment plan in mind.

EVERY DAY WE ENCOUNTER PEOPLE WHO COULD BENEFIT FROM OUR HELP, OUR KINDNESS, AND OUR LOVE.

None of us have any idea how the smallest gesture might make the greatest difference in the life of another. After you look at every situation with your mind, be sure to have another look at it with your heart. Doing the right thing rarely makes financial sense and it often places us in awkward, and even dangerous situations. Don't worry about what's in it for you, the universe had a funny way of keeping the books balanced.

Not every recipe requires leaving things to rest for a few minutes, but it turns out some you need to let things rest for several decades. Like I told you, never skip the resting step – it can make all the difference. Now, stop crying and get out there.

When you look for them, opportunities for kindness, grace and giving are all around you. Seriously, open your eyes and you will see several each day.

For the next week turn down your brain and turn up your heart, and look for opportunities to be an unexpected source of joy.

When your cynical brain tries to tell you that someone does not deserve your kindness or that your actions won't make any difference, ignore it, do the kind thing anyway.

I can't promise you that you'll ever hear the "rest of the story" but simply the idea of knowing that you made a difference (even a tiny one) will do amazing things to you. And for that we can all be grateful.

12 – THE BOX TRICK

My parents are expert practitioners of *The Box Trick*. If you are unfamiliar, I will explain.

The Box Trick is pretty simple actually; it is when you place a small birthday or Christmas gift in a larger box so as to obfuscate, and instill confusion in both the mind and heart of the gift receiver.

So, hypothetically, if I had asked for a really cool pair of Carrera sunglasses for my eighteenth birthday, and after cake and ice cream was consumed, I was presented with a box that was both too large and too heavy; I would feel disappointed and dejected, thinking that this large heavy box must contain something other that what I had so clearly requested.

Upon opening this hypothetically large and heavy box, I found it to contain the very sunglasses I had asked for along with piles of crumpled newspaper and two bricks. Okay, you got me.

Of course over time (as all living things do) *The Box Trick* grew and evolved. The *Reverse Box Trick* is when you're expecting something large and you are presented with an impossibly small box that contains a picture of the large thing. This is mostly used when the large gift is simply too unwieldy to wrap. The *Value Box Trick* is when you stick a Marshall's purchase in a Nordstrom box.

INCIDENTALLY THE VALUE BOX TRICK IS THE ONLY VARIATION THAT IS RARELY REVEALED TO THE GIFT RECIPIENT. IT'S UP TO YOU TO COMPARE THE TAGS WITH THE BOX.

The Double Reverse Box Trick (AKA "The Decoy") is when the box is the right size for what you were hoping for, but does not contain it. Instead it contains something of value, but really boring, like a sweater, underwear, or a couple of ties. After watching you struggle to fake happiness, the gift giver then brings out the thing you were hoping for, sometimes unwrapped, but more often shrouded in yet another variation of *The Box Trick*.

You get the idea, we Nazarians are a little sick-in-the-head, and of course we have an extensive collection of boxes. My mother's mantra: never throw away a "good box."

THE NEW BOX TRICK

In the 1990s I worked in the marketing department of a company called Crest Audio, in Paramus NJ. We were a manufacturer of professional audio equipment, mostly amplifiers and mixing consoles.

In the summer, my job involved going out to concerts where our equipment was being used. I would bring company t-shirts and warranty parts to the roadies, and talk to the engineers about products both current and future. Typically I would get to meet the band and often hang out with them backstage and drink their beer.

I AM NOT MAKING THIS UP;
THIS WAS ACTUALLY MY JOB FOR NEARLY FIVE YEARS.

Most of the summer concerts were at outdoor venues (Jones Beach, Garden State Arts Center, Waterloo Village, etc.). Upon arrival at a concert site, we would have to get the car through the outer gate to get to the backstage area where our "All Access" passes would typically be waiting.

The problem was that our names rarely made it to the list held by the rent-a-cop in the outermost security booth. So, we would show up and have to negotiate through a mess of mispronounced names and walkie-talkie chatter. This was inconvenient and could take a very long time.

One time, we were delivering a replacement amplifier, a 110 lb. monster called the 9001, to a concert at Waterloo Village in Stanhope, NJ (might have been Phish, or Horde, I can't remember, it was 20 years ago). As expected, the outer gate had no knowledge that we were coming, so I said the following to the gatekeeper:

"Do you see that big box in my back seat that says *Professional Power Amplifier?* If I don't get that box backstage and installed in the next 45 minutes there is not going to be a concert tonight. Do you want to be responsible for that?"

An actual Crest Audio amplifier box
Is there anything inside? Does it matter?

We were immediately allowed to pass. As we drove along the fence separating the backstage area from the gathering throngs, my coworker and I looked at each other and giggled at how we couldn't believe how well that just worked. It's not that we got away with anything, they were expecting us backstage and the amplifier was used in the concert that night. However, the amp wasn't mission critical, but the guy with the clipboard didn't know that.

From that day forward, all of us who might ever need it kept an empty amplifier box in our trunk. When we would pull up to the gate, we'd simply point at the box, pitch a little bull that might conjure up images of rioting concertgoers and voila; access granted.

I am not advocating illicit deception. However, *The Box Trick* (both the Nazarian Classic and New varieties) can be very effective tools in life.

Daily we encounter obstacles that inhibit our ability to do our jobs or achieve our goals. They aren't really legitimate obstacles, but they are there nonetheless. The rent-a-cop didn't mean to get in my way, yet there he was, just doing his job.

Some "all access" passes from my Crest Audio days

If you can circumvent these hurdles with a little creative duplicity, and perhaps a bit of whimsy, the world will be all the better for it. But be careful, if you over-use or abuse *The Box Trick*, it has a way of coming back to bite you. You only need attend a Nazarian birthday party to see that.

Take a moment to inventory the most frustrating obstacles you encounter with regularity. Some of them might be unavoidable, but others could be reduced or even eliminated with a little creative thinking.

Instead of focusing negativity on those annoyances, think of them as puzzles to be solved. It might take some time but you will make progress, and when you do, those obstacles turn into little victories each and every time you encounter them.

Stephen S. Nazarian

13 – LIFE WILL FIND A WAY

In the 1993 movie *Jurassic Park*, Jeff Goldblum plays Dr. Ian Malcolm who is a mathematician specializing in something called *Chaos Theory*. Dr. Malcolm is of the opinion that no matter how clever the dinosaur-creating scientists think they are nature is ultimately in charge.

To keep their prehistoric creations under control, the bio-engineers have created all the dinosaurs to be female, thinking that this will prevent them from breeding. In a scene that takes place in the Jurassic Park laboratory, one of the scientists says to Dr. Malcolm, "You're implying that a group composed entirely of female animals will breed?"

DR. MALCOLM REPLIES, "NO, I'M, I'M SIMPLY SAYING THAT LIFE, UH... FINDS A WAY."

Of course he was right, the dinosaurs breed and all hell breaks loose. Despite their best efforts to maintain control, they could not keep life from finding a way.

———————————

Lewis Poppleton was my wife's, mother's father. He lived in Elmira, NY where he raised his family. Lewis fought for our country in World War I, and when the war ended in 1918, he came home from Europe to pick up his life right where he had left it.

During the war, Lewis met many interesting people both in the service, and in the countries where he served. In the years following the war, he would occasionally share stories about his adventures with his family.

THE 1920S CAME AND WENT, AND THEN THE GREAT DEPRESSION HIT.

Lewis Poppleton

One day after returning home from one of the many jobs he held to support his family, he came across an oddly addressed envelope in the mail. It simply said:

> **Lewis Poppleton**
> **New York State**

That was it, nothing more. It turns out that during the war, Lewis had met a man in Europe, and had made quite an impression on him. The man had learned his name, and which of the fifty United States he was from, but little else. Fifteen or so years later, the man had emigrated from Europe and settled in Pennsylvania. He had always been curious about what had become of the American solider that he met in the war, so he wrote a letter and addressed it with the only information he had.

ZIP codes would not come into being for another three decades, so the post office was used to helping the mail find its way with whatever information they had, but this envelope was pretty sparse. They had no Internet, no databases, no connected data of any kind.

Lewis was thrilled to receive the letter, and eventually took his family to visit the man and his family in Pennsylvania. I have no idea if they were ever close, but think about the things that had to happen for that letter to be delivered. That letter wanted to find its way, and it did.

When I went to high school in Penfield New York, our mascot was the "Chief." We were all very proud to be Chiefs, but in the early 2000s, our beloved mascot ran afoul of political correctness and was changed.

SOME TIME IN 2002, THE MIGHTY ATHLETES OF PENFIELD CEASED TO BE CHIEFS AND BEGAN TO BE PATRIOTS.

Looking to make something positive out of the loss of our mascot, three brothers in town decided to do something about it. In 2002, the very first *Penfield Chief Memorial Golf Tournament* was held to raise money for local charities and celebrate our truncated heritage. For years I tried to participate in the tournament, but family and work schedules conspired against me for nearly a decade.

Finally, in 2012, I was able to make it happen and I went to work putting together a foursome.

- My first call was to my brother Doug (Penfield Chief, 1984) who immediately signed on to fly up from Baltimore.

- I then called my sister's husband Russell (Penfield Chief, 1988) who agreed to join us.

- I rounded out the foursome with one of my oldest friends (we met in preschool) Bernard (Penfield Chief, 1987) who thought playing in the tournament was a fine idea.

Here we are sporting our custom hats after 18 holes of, um, golf

It was a crisp fall morning when we climbed aboard our carts and headed out onto the links. The tournament organizers had strategically placed kegs of beer at several locations along the course, and each time we came across one of these sites, we made sure to take full advantage so as to prevent dehydration.

DEHYDRATION CAN BE VERY DANGEROUS.

Somewhere around the eighth hole, I found myself in the position of needing to return some of the aforementioned beer to the earth from whence it came. As uncomfortable as this was, it was a clear sign that I was not dehydrated.

I walked several steps into the woods, and down a small embankment to do what had to be done, with a modicum of privacy. Once I was out of public view, I looked down and saw a golf ball. As a regular supplier of golf balls to the woods, I feel that when I find a ball among the leaves and sticks, I am supposed to pick it up and return it to the field of play.

AH... THE CIRCLE OF LIFE. [INSERT LION KING SONG HERE]

When the deed was done and it was time to return to the fairway, I reached down and picked up the ball. As I pushed some dirt off it with my thumb, I noticed that the ball had some writing on it.

In 1996, my wife Emily's sister Julia gave birth to her first child George M. Dailey. Instead of handing out cigars or sending fancy announcements, Julia and her husband Mike gave out dozens of sleeves of golf balls bearing the name, weight, and birthday of their newborn son.

Finding this ball may at first seem like no big deal, until you find out that at the time of George's birth, Julia and Mike both lived, and gave away all the golf balls; in San Francisco!

Of all the golfers in Rochester NY, I am the only one who would have ever recognized the name of my nephew on a ball. Furthermore, I golf only once or twice a year. So, given where I saw it, the odds of anyone finding that golf ball at all are pretty small. But when you add in the frequency with which I golf, and that I had never set foot on that particular course, it takes things up several orders of magnitude.

My gloved hand holding the curious find

By itself, the discovery of a wayward family golf ball does not bear any great significance, but the meaning of such a thing goes far beyond the simplicity of the encounter.

From science fiction dinosaurs, to friends reunited across continents, to golf balls that travel 2,700 miles all by themselves, we all need to trust that, things that are meant to be will be. For the same reason human beings cannot hold back the ocean nor tame the weather, the things in our lives that are supposed to happen, will, no matter what we do.

In 429 B.C., Sophocles tried to tell us this in the Greek tragedy Oedipus Rex. If you are unfamiliar look it up. No matter how clever you are you can't stop it.

So, stop fighting it and let the things in your life that are meant to be - find a way.

For the longest time I looked at writing as something I did as a part of my job, but I never considered that I could write for a living. I mean, who would pay me to do something that comes easily to me? As a result, I discounted my writing as simply a means an end. All the signs were there, but I simply ignored them. Once I recognized my affinity for writing as something of value, I questioned what took so long.

What are the things in your life that are trying to find a way?

No matter how much you resist them, the things that are meant to be shall be, however with a little help from you they could happen even sooner.

There are hints and clues all around you, but they only matter if you pay attention. What is hiding in the woods alongside the golf course of your life? I recommend you drink a few beers and head in there to find out. After all, you're not going to make it very far if you're dehydrated.

Stephen S. Nazarian

14 – SIGNIFICANT DIGIT AUTO REPAIR

I'm a car guy. I am not going to apologize for it. I like reading about cars, I like driving cars and I like working on cars. If I could have a car collection as diverse and large as my wife's shoe collection – I would.

I have written about car repair before, and I can promise you that I will again before too long. I enjoy working on cars so much that I would rather spend the afternoon replacing the brakes on the family minivan than sit on the couch watching some kind of sporting event.

Now, don't get me wrong, given the choice of working on the minivan or my 1984 "Heart to Heart" convertible I would pick the 380 SL every time, but at the end of the day, any time I can spend fixing, improving, tuning or otherwise caring for a car is, at least to me, time well spent.

MY DAD IS *NOT* A CAR GUY.

The man has a certain pragmatic practicality that manifests itself in many ways. However, his approach to automobiles may be the purest expression of this part of his personality.

In the early 1990s, my parents owned a dark red Ford Taurus sedan. This car replaced the long-loved "brown on rust" Pinto in which my brother, sister and I all learned to drive, but we'll get to that car later.

The Taurus was a practical, reliable car. I wouldn't call it exciting, but I suppose there is some inherent excitement in practicality and reliability, at least that's what my Dad would tell you.

Over the course of seven years or so, the Taurus served our family well. It met with a few mishaps along the way, including an unfortunate encounter with a large rock in the parking lot of my Dad's office building. But, in the end, the car performed as designed, delivering dependable, safe transportation well into six-figures of mileage.

In the twilight months of the Taurus' time in the Nazarian garage, some things transpired that were not mission-critical but required attention. I don't recall exactly what happened, but one of the front turn-signal lenses broke, leaving an inspection-failing hole in the plastic. Knowing the car was "circling the drain" my dad decided to forgo the $100 factory part and fix it himself.

Looking at the problem, and then searching the house, he found a solution. Taking a piece of vinyl carpet protection runner, he cut a shape that matched the curved profile of the broken lens. He trimmed and trimmed until it fit just right and then using clear silicone bathroom caulk, he adhered it to the car.

From a distance you couldn't tell anything was wrong. Close up, you couldn't help but be impressed with how much the piece of carpet protector resembled the look of the original part.

AS A CAR GUY I FIND THIS KIND OF REPAIR ABSOLUTELY APPALLING, BUT IN THIS CASE I CAN'T SAY IT WAS ANYTHING SHORT OF BRILLIANT.

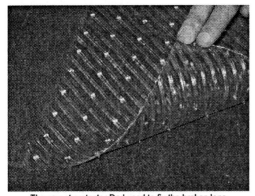

A few months later when my Dad dragged the car into the dealership to trade it in, the valuation guy gave it a quick walk-around and said, "she's pretty tired, but I'm going to give you an extra $100 just because of how awesome that lens repair is." Net savings on the complete hack-job of a repair; $200.

The carpet protector Dad used to fix the broken lens

LARRY NAZARIAN – 1, THE SYSTEM – 0

Growing up in suburbia, we had a tetherball pole in our back yard. Tetherball is pretty much the tic-tac-toe of outdoor sports, in that equally matched players will never produce a meaningful win or loss, but lopsided contests are over almost immediately. That said we enjoyed smacking the ball at each other, and when you were the taller half of a game, it was fun (at least for me) to briefly experience athletic dominance.

Over time, it seemed to us kids that the tetherball pole was getting shorter, but we chalked it up all of us getting taller, and since it was in the middle of the yard, there were really no points of reference to check it against. I suppose we could have grabbed a measuring tape, but it didn't matter that much.

One day we walked back to "the pole" and it was clear that something was amiss. The ball was only about a foot off the ground and the game was essentially unplayable.

We walked away and found something else to do. It was the 1980s, that's what we did.

Later that day at dinner, one of us told my Dad that something had happened to the tetherball pole, and that it had become too short to play. We speculated that perhaps it had sunk into the ground and maybe we could "pull it out."

MY FATHER SAT SILENTLY FOR A FEW MINUTES AND THEN MADE A CONFESSION.

As luck would have it for a guy who had a penchant for "hack-job" car repairs, the diameter of our tetherball pole was exactly the same as the exhaust system on our 1980 Ford Pinto.

Little by little, my Dad had been stealing chunks of our game to repair his car. The day before the big drop, he took a piece more than a foot long.

That was the end of the tetherball era in the Nazarian back yard.

In science there is this idea of "significant digits or figures." The basic concept is that there is a level of detail beyond which additional information is irrelevant. This is similar to the idea in business that sometimes making sure something is finished is more important than making it perfect. In the realm of automobiles, this is something my father has nearly perfected.

As you approach the challenges and puzzles before you, be careful not to work too hard on any one solution. Every effort and resource you don't need to expend can be used on something else; like buying your kids a new tetherball pole.

Tetherball Baby!

In the days to come, pay attention to how precise a particular task or result really needs to be.

Think about it like this: If postage for a letter under one ounce costs $0.49, and a letter weighing over one ounce but under two ounces costs $0.70, all you really need to know is if the letter is over or under the one-ounce mark. It does not matter by how much.

Try and limit your effort and precision to just the right amount, since any more is a waste of your time and will not be appreciated.

Precisely declaring that your letter weighs exactly 1.67 ounces matters not to the postman. All he hears is "more than an ounce" and will then ask you for $0.70.

However, as you find the effort "sweet spot" in things, be careful not to pull back too much. Doing more than is necessary will go unnoticed, but doing not enough will yield a different result entirely.

15 – KEEP TRACK OF YOUR SEEDS

One spring about ten years ago we came home from the garden center with a minivan full of plants, seeds, and mulch for the yard. One of the packets contained seeds for mint. We had been warned to be careful with mint, because it is a very aggressive plant that would take over everything in its path. So, with this in mind, I decided to plant the mint way back in the wooded area of our yard, along the fence where nothing meaningful grows.

A few months later on a hot Saturday afternoon, my wife asked if we had the makings for mojitos. I said we did, but I would need to go get some mint. "What about the mint you planted?" she said.

I had completely forgotten about the mint I had planted back in the woods. I went out to the back part of the yard looking on the ground along the fence line where I had planted the seeds. I didn't see anything. I walked up and down the area where I was certain I had planted the seeds, but still couldn't find any mint – though I swore I could smell it.

Only when I lifted my gaze up off the ground did I realize what had happened. Right in front of me were a dozen, four-foot tall mint plants. I had been looking at the ground for mint leaves, but all I had seen were the trunks of the now giant mint plants.

I HAD FORGOTTEN ABOUT THE SEEDS I HAD PLANTED, AND THEY HAD GROWN OUT OF CONTROL.

When my wife's father was still alive, we had a tradition for every visit to my in-laws home in Virginia. One morning of every visit, my wife, daughter and mother-in-law would drive into town for pedicures. About an hour later my father-in-law, my three boys and I would drive into town and spend an hour at a playground, before meeting the girls for lunch.

The last time we did this, was in 2010, it was a bright sunny day and I brought our camera to the park, hoping to get some good shots of the boys while they played.

After playing on several different playground pieces, they went over to the swings. Since it was such a sunny day I decided to experiment with some fast shutter speeds. As they pumped their legs up and down, pushing the swings to their limit, I talked them through the safe way to leap from a swing.

There is a place in the arc of a swing where the forces just about toss you out. If you leap at the right time, you can safely fly about twenty feet and land on your feet; it is quite a thrill.

Lewis and Oliver defy gravity with the help of a fast shutter

Once they had mastered the technique, I got several great shots of each of them flying through the air. Each time they swung, they jumped and they landed safely. When we were done, we met the girls for lunch and that was that.

On an early Saturday evening in spring 2014, we were entertaining about thirty of my wife's coworkers at our home, to celebrate the graduation of two Intensive Care Fellows. There were some kids along at the party, and after they had eaten dinner they went down the hill the schoolyard behind our house.

They were playing on the playground equipment, which included swings. My son Lewis (who was just shy of is thirteenth birthday) decided to swing as high as he could, and jump. When he released, he got a bit off kilter and as he landed, he put his arms out to brace his fall.

As he hit the ground, his left elbow made a crunching noise and in his words,

"MY ELBOW LOOKED A LITTLE FUNNY, SO I TWISTED IT AROUND UNTIL IT LOOKED NORMAL AGAIN."

Over the next twenty-four hours we enjoyed six hours in the emergency room, x-rays, consultation with several doctors, an overnight stay in the pediatric ward, a two-hour surgery, recovery, a blue, full-arm cast, discharge, and a trip home via the pharmacy for pain medicine.

Lewis broke the head of his radius bone where it meets the elbow, and he did it in such a way that it took a Pediatric Orthopedic Surgeon two hours to put it back in place.

At one point in the ordeal I asked him what he was thinking jumping off the swing like that. He looked right at me and said, "I was just doing what you taught me to do that day in the park with Granddad."

ONCE AGAIN, I HAD PLANTED A SEED AND NEGLECTED TO KEEP AN EYE ON IT.

When I taught Lewis (and his brothers) how to jump out of a swing, they were only strong enough to leap when the forces were just right and safe. As the swing passes the safe zone, the forces at play make it much harder to jump out.

In the years since, Lewis has grown much stronger, not to mention he is a legitimate Isshin-Ryu Karate black belt. When I asked for more details on how he jumped from the swing, he described that he had jumped higher and later than I had showed him. He wasn't doing it to disobey me, he was doing it because it was higher; and he could.

AS THE NURSE IN PRE-OP SAID TO US BOTH… BOYS WILL BE BOYS.

When I had planted the seed of swing jumping in my boys, things were safe and predictable. I never gave it another thought. But while I wasn't paying attention, the circumstances changed, making what I taught them no longer such a good idea.

I'm not saying that Lewis' broken arm was my fault. Certainly a thirteen-year-old boy is capable of exercising some judgment.

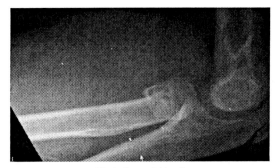
The broken radial head

But it does make you think about how the things you say and do have a life, long after you say and do them. I had a customer ask me once if the software we were programming for him would be "forward compatible" with operating systems and browsers coming out in the future. Of course (after suppressing both an appalled look and snorting laugh) I told him that there is no such thing as "forward compatibility."

The fact is that we have no idea what the future holds, so we would be wise to keep an eye on the seeds we plant. I have learned that many will require adjustments, and that it is okay to jump in and make changes as needed. If you're lucky, you just might keep one more elbow from making a crunching noise. But if you miss it, at least you'll have plenty of mint for your mojitos – and you're probably going to need it.

Do you teach or give advice? Have you ever had something thrown back at you in changed circumstances?

For the next seven days, every time you assume someone (for whom you are responsible) knows what he or she is doing, ask them to verify what they know to be true. You may quickly find some discrepancies between your assumptions and theirs.

Now is not the time to stop planting seeds. Now is the time to start keeping track of them.

---

16 – DOLLAR STORE GOOFBALL

I graduated from college in May 1991, I was twenty-two. Having been born at the end of 1968, my twenties lined up almost perfectly with the nineties. In January 1992, I moved to Manhattan.

Living and working in and around New York City, you would think that a vibrant and active social life would be easy to come by, but a funny thing happens when twelve million people all live within a twenty-mile circle; they don't really talk to each other.

> **WHAT'S WORSE, I'M A GOOFBALL.**
> **I HAVE A TENDENCY TO GET OVEREXCITED ABOUT MOST THINGS AND SOME PEOPLE FIND THAT, WELL, OFF-PUTTING.**

I came to New York in a long-distance relationship, which did not survive the first year. After that I went on a series of random dates from a variety of sources.

Internet dating was in its infancy, but being an adventuresome fellow, and fairly tech savvy, I figured it couldn't hurt to try.

It was so early in the days of "match.com" that pictures were not part of the equation. As a result, you were completely beholden to the other person's skills as a writer for an accurate description. I did learn one important lesson early on:

> **IN THE DROP DOWN MENU WHERE YOU GET TO SELECT BODY TYPE, "ATHLETIC" ALMOST ALWAYS MEANT THAT HER SPORT WAS EITHER THE SHOT PUT, OR THE CLEAN-AND-JERK.**

Because the set up at the time was just the electronic version of a blind date without the mutual friend, I would arrange to meet someone for a drink after work. If that went well, perhaps we'd move on to dinner. If the drink was a disaster, then, "I've got to get home, I have an early meeting tomorrow." We didn't have cell phones, so the "rescue call" was not yet an option.

On one date, we had agreed to meet in the lobby of her office building. Now, I am a little more than 6' 2" but since the form on the dating site didn't allow for half-inches, I rounded up and listed myself as 6' 3". She on the other hand was 6' 4" but being a really tall woman had rounded down, and had also listed herself as 6' 3". When we met in the marble-clad lobby of her 6th Avenue office tower, it was immediately clear we had both lied.

There was another date where I met the young lady at the train station and we proceeded to a bar in SOHO. It was crowded, so it took us almost half an hour to make our way to the bar and get two drinks. She had huge mop of curly blonde hair, and seemed nice enough, but I was picking up an odd vibe from the conversation. I couldn't quite put my finger on it, but I was getting the sense that my first meeting tomorrow morning was getting earlier by the minute.

We finally got two drinks, me with a gin and tonic and she with a Sambuca. We sipped and chatted as best we could over the din of the crowded bar. As she drank, a piece of her hair kept getting caught in the corner of her mouth. The stickiness of the Sambuca was only making the situation worse.

After several rounds of watching her sip her drink and then have to pull the same curly tuft of hair out of her mouth she burst out, "Arrrgh, I hate my hair!"

BEING THE LOGICAL PERSON THAT I AM, I REPLIED, "WELL YOU COULD CUT YOUR HAIR."

Upon hearing this, her eyes locked straight onto mine, and stroking her curls like a James Bond villain with a Siamese cat, she softly said, "I couldn't ever cut my hair, I LOVE MY HAIR!"

Check please!

So, after a series of Internet dates that rarely went beyond a hopeful dinner, a friend of mine suggested that I should meet someone he knew.

This friend played on two different recreational ice hockey teams in Manhattan and one of them was coed. He had a teammate named Laura, and he thought we would really hit it off. Finally, a connection that was more than a series of half-truths on a website.

I went to one of his hockey games and saw them both play. After the game he introduced me to Laura and she was both pretty and seemed very nice. Despite her hockey-playing ways, I would not have described her as "athletic."

A few days later I gave her a call and we talked on the phone for the better part of an hour. She had grown up as the child of college professor parents, and now worked on the management side of a major retailer. She liked hockey because it reminded her of playing with her brothers as a child and she said that, "it keeps me from killing my idiot coworkers, I can always just take my frustrations out on the ice."

All in all we hit it off pretty well, and in the course of our conversation, she mentioned that she had always wanted a pair of diamond earrings, but had yet to get her hands on a pair. The conversation ended with us arranging a date for the coming Saturday. I would pick her up at her apartment and we planned to go out to dinner. I was to pick the restaurant.

AS THE WEEKEND DREW CLOSER I BEGAN TO GET RATHER EXCITED AND MY GOOFBALL WAYS WERE COMING TO THE SURFACE.

The more I thought about our conversation the more I kept dwelling on her desire to have a pair of diamond earrings. Of course I had neither the means nor the inclination to purchase even the cheapest pair of real diamond earrings, but facts like that had never discouraged me before.

Since I worked in Paramus NJ, there were seven malls I could browse on my lunch hour looking for what I needed. My clever idea was to find a pair of diamond-shaped earrings and present them to Laura during our dinner.

I went from store to store looking for earrings in a diamond shape, or even playing card themed earrings with the diamond suit on them. After two full lunch hours of shopping I was still coming up empty and it was Friday, the date was tomorrow. I poked my head into a dollar store on my walk back to my car, and as I looked at the rack of very sad, every-shape-but-diamond, earrings I heard something. Playing on the overhead speakers was a very familiar song, and it provided me with the epiphany I had been seeking.

I PURCHASED A $1 PAIR OF PLAIN, 1.5 INCH ROUND EARRINGS AND WENT BACK TO WORK.

When I got back to the office I dug through the box of CDs under my desk and found exactly what I was looking for. I took the CD case into the copy room, and made two copies using the reduction feature. I then went back to my desk, and using only my scissors and a glue stick, I finished my masterpiece.

Saturday evening came and I drove my little green Saturn through the Lincoln Tunnel to pick up Laura. Living in Manhattan without a car, she was excited to take a ride in a car that wasn't a cab.

I had made reservations at a restaurant called Shanghai Reds, which was at the end of a pier in Weehawken New Jersey. I know it does not sound very nice, but if you know where Weehawken is, then you know that looking out the end of a pier there basically gives you a panoramic view of the Manhattan skyline.

ALL OF THE TABLES FACED THE WINDOWS.
IT WAS LIKE EATING INSIDE A POSTCARD.

We had a nice dinner and the conversation was almost as interesting as the view. I thought for sure this could at least lead to a second date.

When we got back in my car I said, "Oh, I got something for you." I then reached into my glove compartment and retrieved a little box, wrapped plainly with newsprint, and a bow drawn on with red Sharpie.

Laura smiled but seemed a little uncomfortable. She opened the box, to find what I had made for her… the world's very first pair of Neil Diamond earrings.

A Photoshop reenactment of the infamous Neil Diamond earrings

I thought I had been the most clever, thoughtful and romantic guy ever. I later found out through our mutual friend, that Laura thought it was both goofy, and a little creepy. The second date never happened.

Years later when I met my wife Emily, we were separated by 300 miles, with her in Rochester and me in New York. She didn't have email, so I wrote her letters, lots of letters.

Since I was freelancing at the time, I would sit in my home office and write to her about what I was doing, what I was thinking, what music I was listening to, what my dogs were doing, what I had for lunch and all sorts of other goofball stuff going through my mind. At the time, these seemed like perfectly appropriate letters to be sending to this pretty pediatrician that I was falling for.

Several years after we got married we went out to dinner for our anniversary, and out of her purse she pulled a stack of those letters bound together with a ribbon. She untied the pile and started reading. As my own words crossed the restaurant table and reentered my brain, all I could think was, "good god, what a goofball I was."

The same guy, who made a seemingly nice girl uncomfortable with a pair of homemade Neil Diamond earrings, helped another girl fall in love with him through a series of equally goofy letters.

WHAT WAS THE DIFFERENCE? THE AUDIENCE.

Always be yourself. If you're inclined to be goofy, be goofy. If you're a nerd, be nerdy. My Grandpa Carlson used to say, "if you marry for money, you'll earn every penny." A corollary to this wisdom would be:

Don't change who you are just to be liked. If you manage to pull it off, you'll be forced to be that person for the rest of your life.

God made you who you are for a reason. Be the best version of that person you can, and you will find someone who will love you for it.

Do you hold back on who you really are? Stop it. Starting today, be the person that comes naturally, no matter how odd it may feel, or how unconventional others might consider it.

Certainly we must temper our behavior for certain situations, but for the most part you should always be yourself. When you do this, those drawn to you will truly appreciate the unique being that you are, and you will be happy ever after.

Stephen S. Nazarian

17 – SAY THANK YOU TO EVERYONE

In January 2014 I had to fly to Los Angeles for work. It was one of those really quick trips where I left Rochester NY on a Friday afternoon, got to LA at midnight pacific time, did my work thing on Saturday and then took the red-eye back, getting home before noon Sunday. 6,000 miles is a long way to go for a 2-hour meeting, but we all must do what we must.

When I arrived at the airport on Friday afternoon I went straight to security since I had no bag to check, and I already had my boarding pass. As I entered the security labyrinth, there was a TSA worker at the entrance hunched over an iPad mounted to a pole. He briefly glanced up at me and asked me to wait.

The TSA Randomizer

After about thirty seconds, he stood up, looked at me and said, "All set." He then tapped the iPad, a large arrow appeared on screen and he looked at me again and, pointing in the same direction as the arrow and said, "Go that way." I looked him straight in the eye and said, "thank you." A smile came across his face and he said, "you're most welcome, this thing (the iPad) is stupid – nobody says thank you."

I have since learned that the iPad app he was using is something called the TSA randomizer. In Rochester where we have only two or three lines it seems completely pointless, but such are government regulations. I would really love to find out what the TSA paid to program an app that randomly displays a left or right arrow. I know plenty of programmers who could do that in less time than it takes a large cup of coffee to go cold, but I digress.

As I walked away from the TSA agent and his silly app, it occurred to me that although we generally live and operate in a polite society, a small increase in gratitude could have a massive effect. So for the duration of my trip I undertook a completely non-scientific study, focused on a conscious increase in my gratitude for everyone I would encounter. Since is it very easy to be a crabby son-of-a-bitch while traveling, this seemed like it would be both fun and interesting.

I set out to look everyone in the eye and thank him or her for whatever it was they were doing. Rather quickly I realized my own standard of behavior had me thanking only those with whom I interacted directly, a counter agent, food vendor, or flight attendant. By opening my eyes just a little more I found dozens of opportunities to go a step further in my gratitude of those around me.

- I thanked a worker changing a bag in a garbage can into which I tossed an empty coffee cup.

- I thanked the lady whose job it is to stand next to the shuttle bus at the Philadelphia airport and say, "Watch your step." No joke that is what she does all day long, because on my return trip I saw her again and I asked her.

- I thanked the guy running the taxi stand at LAX even though he was acting like a jerk.

- I thanked the lady at the CVS in LA that did not have the thing I was looking for.

- I thanked two LA city workers who were painting street light poles on a Saturday morning. As I was walking by I looked up at them on their ladders and shouted "thank you!" The one guy looked down and sarcastically (thinking I was some kind of cynical a-hole) and said, "For what?" I replied with a smile, "For working on a Saturday." He had nothing to say in reply other than a smile and a nod.

- I bought a Mexican style breakfast on the street in LA and I thanked the guy at the window, and then made sure to stick my head in the window and thank the cook too.

THERE IS A WEALTH OF RESEARCH ON THE VALUE OF APPRECIATION.

In the book *The Carrot Principle* by Adrian Gostick and Chester Elton, they point out:

The fact is that 79 percent of employees who quit their jobs cite a lack of appreciation as the key reason for leaving. Sixty-five percent of

North Americans report that they weren't recognized in the least bit the previous year.

These few statistics explain why even the slightest acknowledgement of someone's value is met with a greater response than if you'd simply walked up and handed them a twenty-dollar-bill.

When I approached the Philly Shuttle Bus Lady to ask her about her job, she first gave me the stink-eye. But once she realized that my interest in her and her job was sincere, she smiled and opened up immediately. I asked her how often people trip even though she says, "watch your step?" She wryly replied, "About a thousand times a day." She said that people trip all the time and she is pretty sure nobody hears her anyway. I didn't know what to say, other than thanking her again for what she does.

Many business books have been written to address this subject, but very few managers actually follow the advice.

Margie Warrell, an author, speaker and Forbes Magazine contributor sums up this subject nicely in a piece called *Feeling Appreciated? Why It Can Make All The Difference.* Get on the Google and search, it should be easy to find.

You know that warm feeling you have watching a loved one opening and appreciating a gift you thoughtfully chose for them on a cozy Christmas morning? You can have that feeling all day, every day; all you have to do is say THANK YOU – to everyone.

Here is the challenge – for the next week say thank you to everyone you encounter. Don't limit yourself to those with whom you interact with directly, take it to the next level. Seek out people who are making a difference or even just doing their job and let them know that you noticed and appreciate them.

Gratitude is contagious and before you know it, not only will you be changing lives around you, but you'll begin to see a real change in yourself.

Stephen S. Nazarian

18 – A LIGHT IN THE WELL

In November 1995 I purchased my first house in Greenwood Lake, NY. In real estate terms I purchased what is known as a *Handyman Special.* I will not go into all the things wrong with the house when I bought it (even I would get bored with that) but one thing was a huge challenge, from the get-go, was the plumbing.

I spent the first weekend in the crawlspace, on my back, with my Dad, replacing all the old, rusted galvanized steel pipes with copper. It was a mess.

One of the things my house had, with which I had almost no experience at all, was a well. I generally understood how it worked, but for my entire life I had enjoyed the reliability of municipal water. In the beginning, apart from some pressure variations, I found the well to be as reliable as city-water, until…

I am a morning person. In fact as I write this, both the sun and the balance of my family are still more than an hour from rising. So, when I arose early one cold morning in January 1996, I expected to make a pot of coffee, enjoy a hot shower and head off to work. I went to the sink, filled my coffee pot, but as I finished, it seemed like the water pressure was dropping more than it should. I turned on the coffee and hopped into the shower. I had just managed to fully shampoo my hair when the water slowed to a trickle and then stopped completely.

FOR THOSE WHO ARE UNFAMILIAR, A WELL IS MADE UP OF BASICALLY THREE THINGS:

1. A hole in the ground

2. A pump

3. A pressure tank.

If the well is shallow (fewer than forty feet) the pump can ***pull*** the water up to the surface, but if it is deeper, the pump is actually at the bottom of the well from which it ***pushes*** the water up out of the ground.

MY WELL WAS EIGHTY-FIVE FEET DEEP.

The pressure tank acts as a buffer since water coming directly from a pump is slow to get going, and can deliver inconsistent pressure. So, the pump fills up the pressure tank and when you open a faucet, the pressure in the tank instantly, and smoothly delivers the water. When the pressure in the tank drops below a defined point, a pressure-switch turns on the pump and the whole cycle repeats. The making of my coffee and the first 90 seconds of my shower had emptied the tank, but the pump could not re-fill the tank because:

THE TOP OF MY WELL WAS FROZEN.

With shampoo filled hair I dried off, got dressed and headed outside to see what I could do about the problem. My well was poorly designed. The top of the hole-in-the-ground was about four feet from the foundation of the house. The pipe came out of the ground, took a 90-degree turn and traveled the four feet to the crawlspace inside a concrete channel. This lateral pipe was pretty much at ground level (not below the frost line like it should be), and exposed to the cold of the air. Covering this whole setup was a single piece of un-insulated, half-inch plywood.

KNOWING WHAT I KNOW NOW, IT IS CLEAR THAT THIS WELL WAS GOING TO FREEZE; IT WAS JUST A QUESTION OF THE TEMPERATURE. THAT MORNING, I LEARNED THAT THE ANSWER WAS SOMEWHERE AROUND 15° F.

As I gazed ignorantly at my icy well by flashlight, shampoo freezing in my hair, I decided to take an extreme approach, thawing the pipe with a blowtorch. Ten minutes later I was back in the shower continuing with my day, but I knew the issue was far from resolved.

As I worked through my day I thought, I figured, I researched (as much as one could back then without Google) and I annoyed my engineering coworkers looking for answers.

By day's end the best I had come up with was one of those heat wires that people zigzag along their rooflines to prevent ice dams. I purchased the shortest one Home Depot had (50 ft), and wrapped it all around the pipe and tacked some insulation to the backside of the plywood cover.

For three weeks the well flowed freely, but when I got my next electric bill I realized that leaving a device rated at 1,200 watts plugged in 24/7 was a pricey proposition.

I NEEDED TO HEAT THE TOP OF MY WELL, CONSISTENTLY, BUT INEXPENSIVELY. UGH!

The day I got the electric bill I was on the phone with my parents. As I told my story, my mom reminded me about a trick her dad had used to keep his well from freezing. My mother grew up in Bradford PA. If you ever watch the national news in the morning, Bradford is often noted as the coldest place in the country, so they know a little but about freezing wells.

What my grandfather had done was so simple and so obvious (once you saw it), but it was counter-intuitive. We've all had a light bulb blowout while we are doing something, so we immediately go get a new bulb and foolishly grab the blown one – and it is HOT!

Using this information to his advantage, my grandfather had simply wired up a 100-watt light bulb near the top of his well and it never froze. He would flip it on in the fall and off in the spring.

THE ELECTRICITY TO RUN THE BULB COST HIM A COUPLE OF BUCKS A MONTH. A SMALL PRICE TO PAY FOR FREE FLOWING WATER.

So, the next day I unplugged my fifty-foot heat wire and replaced it with a light bulb. At first I used a 100W bulb, but after some experimenting and temperature measurement I concluded that a 40W would do. My well never froze again and I reduced the cost of keeping it that way by 97%.

The pharmaceutical industry has a term: *Off Label Use*. Pretty dull I know, but what is really means is:

We designed a drug to do one thing, and it turns out one of the side-effects is in fact something useful, so we won't bother to get it approved for that use, but nudge-nudge, wink-wink we won't keep it a secret either.

In the software business they like to say, "That's not a flaw, it's a feature," same thing.

The value here is simple, but tricky to apply. I could have tapped hundreds of resources looking for an appropriate heat source for my well, but I never would have come across "light bulb." Why? Because light bulbs are for light (but they happen also to produce heat).

The subtitle of the blog I started writing in 2014 (and that led to this book) was "Answers hiding in plain sight." It doesn't get much more obvious than (literally) a light bulb going off in front of you. Now go forth and look beyond… everything.

As you go about your business, and consume information about all kinds of things this week, make a point to look beyond the primary purpose of a thing, and take in everything that it actually does.

It might not bear fruit immediately, but one day you'll find an answer right there in the unwritten, "off label use" of something. When it happens, but sure to imagine a light bulb lighting up just above your head, not because it matters, but because it's fun.

19 – SOMETIMES TOO MUCH IS TOO MUCH

Flamboyant on-again, off-again VanHalen front-man David Lee Roth has often been credited with proclaiming that:

TOO MUCH IS NEVER ENOUGH.

Similarly, Irish writer and poet Oscar Wilde is famous for opining:

MODERATION IS FATAL, NOTHING SUCCEEDS LIKE EXCESS.

Given the extroverted, and performance-focused nature of these two showmen, it is easy to understand why both of them would take these public positions. However, I have found that in most cases, too much is, as you might expect, in fact, too much.

I love music. I have always had an affinity for music of all kinds and from the day I purchased a vinyl LP copy of Kansas' *Point Of No Return* from the J.M. Fields store, in Panorama Plaza, in Penfield, NY, I have been a collector of music.

I collected records and then cassette tapes. By the time CDs became the common music medium, I was at the point in my life where I was making enough money to really build a meaningful music collection. At the high watermark I think I owned more than 750 CDs.

THEN CAME ITUNES.

I was an early adopter of computer-based music libraries, sitting every evening for more than six months loading my CDs into the computer. In the years following I have continued to load and purchase music at a regular clip to the point where my collection of music now measures more than fifty-five days.

I COULD START PLAYING MY ITUNES LIBRARY ON NEW YEAR'S DAY AND I WOULDN'T REPEAT A SINGLE SONG UNTIL SOME TIME AROUND THE FIRST OF MARCH.

This sounds like a wonderful thing, right? I have thousands of choices from Vivaldi, to the aforementioned VanHalen, but there is a problem. I pull up the library to play something and I end up scrolling and clicking for quite some time, often thinking there is nothing I want to listen to. I pick something, I start listening and within a song or two I feel the urge to pick something else. I am constantly haunted by the idea that I could be doing better.

> **WHAT SHOULD BE A THOROUGHLY SATISFYING EXPERIENCE ENDS UP BEING JUST THE OPPOSITE.**

In the late 1990s I worked for a computer-consulting firm in Manhattan. One of my better customers was a VP of operations for a large NY bank, and his job was to oversee process analysis and engineering. I had several consultants and analysts working with him.

One day he told me about a recent success his team had achieved. They had been called into a check-processing center because the throughput of the operation was not meeting expectations. In the center of the operation were five, giant IBM 3890 check scanning machines. IBM had been consulted on the situation and their recommendation had been that the bank purchase two additional 3890s at a cost of ~$1Million each. The bank was dubious, so they called my customer in for a second opinion.

An IBM 3890 in action

His team collected all the data from the processing operation and plugged it into a special analysis software package they used in situations just like this. After the analysis was complete, the team returned to the check-processing center with the following recommendation:

- Re-arrange some of the workers across several of the stations in the process
- Unplug two of the 3890s

In the end, the problem with the process was not insufficient capacity, but rather excess capacity. The five 3890s were too demanding and they were throwing off every other part of the process. Net savings to the bank: the $2 million they didn't have to spend on new equipment plus the liberation of $2 million worth of equipment that could be re-purposed elsewhere.

ALL TOO OFTEN WE ASSUME THAT IF SOME MEASURE OF SOMETHING IS GOOD, THEN A GREATER MEASURE OF THAT SAME THING IS BETTER. THE TRUTH IS VERY OFTEN THE OPPOSITE.

Not long ago I was visiting my brother in Baltimore and I spent the weekend playing records from his collection of vinyl. He has maybe fifty records.

What's interesting is I had a far more satisfying musical experience with his turntable, than I've had with my iTunes library in years. I have since decided to go through my collection alphabetically by album, disciplining myself to completely finish an album before moving on to the next. I bet I will find some great stuff in there that I've forgotten about.

The psychologist Barry Schwartz covers this entire topic brilliantly in his book *The Paradox of Choice: Why More Is Less.* Lucky for you he summarizes it all nicely in a twenty-minute TED talk which you can easily Google and watch any time.

AS HUMAN BEINGS WE ALL WANT CHOICES, WE ALL WANT OPTIONS, BUT TRUE HAPPINESS LIES SOMEWHERE BETWEEN ARRANGED MARRIAGES, AND GIANT ITUNES LIBRARIES.

Our own personal sweet spot is something we each need to determine for ourselves.

How much of your life is obscured by too much choice? It could be 200+ channels of HDTV yielding nothing worth watching, or one of those new fountain soda machines with a touch screen and more than a hundred drink choices.

Once a day for the next week, make a choice to walk away from choice. Dig out an old mix tape and listen to all of it, even the songs you regret putting on there. Remove all the magazines from your bathroom except for one, but read that one cover to cover.

You will soon discover that there is little value in the availability of choice, but much to be taken from the choices you make. This is definitely one of those areas where quality trumps quantity. Choose wisely my friends, choose wisely.

20 – IT'S ONLY A RACE

I ran my first road race the summer after seventh grade. It was a flat, four-miler in the town where I grew up, and I was sore for days after.

Since then I have probably averaged three road races a year, mostly 5Ks, but a few 10Ks, and some odd distances in between. Doing the math, I figure that I have participated in around 100 road races.

CERTAINLY FEWER THAN SOME, BUT I'D LIKE TO THINK I'VE SEEN A THING OR TWO, POUNDING ALONG THE WHITE LINE OF STREETS, "CLOSED TO TRAFFIC."

One summer my daughter Charlotte and I showed up for a race, a few towns over from where our family had rented a beach house in Rhode Island. In the end, we came home with much more than a t-shirt, and post-race banana.

One of the things I have always liked about running as a sport is that all you need are your shoes and some time. Pretty much anywhere you go, you can find a safe place to run.

Racing is the same. If you can find a race, all you need to do is show up, fill out a form, pay the fee and get ready to run. It is fun to be the runner nobody expected, in a town other than your own, but the flipside of that coin is that someone unexpected can always show up at one of your regular races, where you think you've got the field all figured out.

Several weeks before leaving for vacation we looked up races near our beach destination in Narragansett RI. We found one that looked good, "The Rhody Run For The Troops." It was a 5K, it was 15 miles away from where we'd be staying, and the course ran through a military base (think flat). Even better, the race was to be a fundraiser for a group that sends care packages to troops overseas. Win, win, win, win!

I had planned to sign us up weeks before, but sometimes that sort of thing gets lost in the shuffle of life. So, Saturday afternoon after seven hours in a minivan with four kids and marginal air conditioning, Charlotte turned to me and said, "what time is our race tomorrow?" Oh crap.

I HOPPED ON MY LAPTOP, FOUND THE RACE AND SIGNED US UP. LUCKILY, THE RACE HAD A LATE START, 10:00AM.

Sunday morning, we got up and drove to the race. Since we didn't know where we were going, we left plenty of time to get lost. We arrived a little after 9:00 and the scene looked like most other road races an hour before the gun. We shuffled up to the registration table where, despite having signed up only sixteen hours before, they had our names. We got our numbers, signed the waivers and turned to check out the competition.

The field looked small. With forty-five minutes to go there were maybe a hundred runners and none of them looked like ringers. We wandered around sizing up the opposition, and at one point asked to see a course map; they didn't have one.

Over three decades of road racing here are the things I've learned about the other runners at a race:

Not a threat	People to be careful of
Anyone wearing headphones	Someone who shows up with only minutes to spare
People wearing fully coordinated outfits	Anyone who appears to be a member of a non-scholastic running club or team
People wearing the t-shirt they just got at the registration table	Skinny guys with no shirt (no matter how old)
People wearing the shirt from the same race last year	Well worn running shoes
Anyone wearing denim cut-offs	Anyone who looks fit, and is keeping to themselves, not talking to anyone

OTHER THAN THE WELL-WORN RUNNING SHOES, CHARLOTTE AND I EXHIBITED NONE OF THE QUALITIES LISTED ABOVE.

Ten minutes before 10:00am, they called all the runners to an area near the starting line for "race instructions." This may sound like a good idea, but it is unusual. In fact I don't ever remember being given "race instructions" before. As we listened I guesstimated that there were now 150 runners.

They welcomed everyone, explained the reason for the race, and very briefly described the course. They said that there were marshals on the course at every turn, wearing orange vests. And then they specifically said, **"So, if you pass an intersection and there is no marshal, DO NOT TURN."** All, pretty standard stuff.

The only directional sign I saw all day

They called us to the line, but then something weird happened. Charlotte and I walked right up to the front, placing the toes of our well-worn shoes on the fresh, white, slightly crooked, spray painted line, but nobody joined us.

Normally there are plenty of runners who think they belong up front, and some of them actually do, but everyone in this race wanted to hang back a little. It was very unsettling.

> *SINCE WE WERE ON AN AIR FORCE BASE, THEY UNDERSTANDABLY DID NOT WANT TO USE A GUN TO START THE RACE, SO THEY RANG A COWBELL AND WE WERE OFF.*

With nobody else on the line, Charlotte and I quickly took the lead. We settled into a nice pace. I wasn't wearing a watch, but it felt like about 6:30/mile. We got to the first intersection, where the road we were on ended in a tee, but I saw no marshal. Just as we got to the intersection a guy screeched up in a black pickup truck, jumped out and directed us to turn right.

We ran through the first mile, passing a few intersections, none of which had marshals stationed, so per the instructions given we continued on. We encountered a foursome of golfers crossing the road with their clubs on pull carts. I invited them to join us – they declined.

We rounded a long curve that allowed me to peek off to my left and see where the other runners were. Charlotte was about 50 yards behind me and the next runner was easily 300 yards behind her.

I haven't been the leader in a race of 100+ people since high school, so with more than half of the race to go, I began working on my mental approach for staying out in front.

One generally accepted rule for leading is: don't look back. You have to assume at all times they are right behind you, however you still have physical limits, so the trick is to force yourself to operate at the edge of your physical capabilities and hope they don't catch you. From what I had just seen, I wasn't too worried about being caught, but I did want to turn in a decent time.

I felt good, and I was glad Charlotte was keeping up and would likely be the female winner and number two overall; and then I heard it.

FROM OFF IN THE DISTANCE BEHIND ME SOMEONE YELLED, "YOU-MISSED-THE- TURN!"

Slowing down and pivoting on my heels I saw a very discouraging site. A little more than a quarter mile back, the rest of the runners were turning left onto a road that first ten or so runners had blown right past. There had been no marshal, so we didn't turn.

I immediately turned and started running back. However, when you just spent the past ninety seconds figuring out how to mentally keep up as the leader in the race, it is devastating to your psyche to realize that not only are you now in 50th place, but also that your 5K is going to be more like 3.6 miles, not the 3.1 you were counting on.

By the time I got back to the turn where there had been no marshal, I was behind runners with jogging strollers and a few people who were walking. Oh boy was I pissed.

AS I ROUNDED THE CORNER JOINING THE STREAM OF OTHER RUNNERS, THE NOW PRESENT MARSHAL ISSUED A SINCERE, BUT SHEEPISH "SORRY MAN."

For the next mile my mind was exploding. I thought of all the things I could say when I finally crossed the line in whatever place I'd end up. After calming down a little, I decided I would tell them, "the first rules of organizing a road race were to make a course map available, have the course well labeled, and to have the marshals stationed before the race went off." Yeah, I was going to tell them.

But as I ran the last mile, I calmed down even more. I passed more parents pushing jogging strollers, I passed service men and women in short haircuts wearing t-shirts emblazoned with their unit insignia. I passed several women who appeared to be spouses or girlfriends of soldiers that could not run the race because they were overseas serving our country.

WHEN I FINALLY CROSSED THE LINE WITH A TIME I WILL NOT DISCLOSE, I HAD DECIDED THAT IT WAS IN FACT "JUST A RACE."

The finish line - no, that was not my time

The race organizers were beside themselves. They were upset, embarrassed, and really didn't know what to do. They kept coming up to us and apologizing, we kept saying, "it's just a race."

We grabbed a couple of waters and sat in the shade, deciding, although winning would have been fun, the story we now had to tell was probably better.

A few minutes later the race director called "all the runners who ran extra" over to the registration table... there were maybe ten of us. The first thing he did was offer to refund the $20 we had all paid to run the race. We unanimously declined citing that it was a fundraiser and that the money should stay. He then turned to Charlotte and me and said, "is there anyone here who does not agree that despite the screw-up, that these two are the male and female winners of our race today." Again the response of the group was unanimous. He apologized again for the problems and said that they would be announcing awards once all the runners were in.

CHARLOTTE AND I HAD SOME OF THE FOOD THAT WAS PROVIDED, DRANK SOME MORE WATER AND WATCHED OTHER RUNNERS BOTH YOUNG AND OLD CROSS THE LINE

When the time came for awards, the Unit Commander from the base said a few words thanking everyone on behalf of all those the money raised would be helping.

AFTER ALL THAT HAD HAPPENED, HONESTLY THAT WAS ENOUGH FOR ME.

Then the race director took the microphone. After explaining to the crowd what had happened, they awarded the second place male and female awards, envelopes containing some amount of cash. They then called up "Mike," the guy who had been the actual first person across the line. They explained that when he finished, he refused to hand the official the tear-off part of his number saying, "I might be here first, but I didn't win this race." They gave him an envelope too.

Me & Charlotte - post race, pre awards

Charlotte and I were introduced as a "father and daughter" team and they called us up together, declaring us the male and female winners, and handing us each an envelope. It was both a good and strange feeling. While I appreciated the way they handled it, it didn't feel completely right being declared the winner. No times were mentioned.

Before we left, Charlotte and I went and talked to Mike, the guy who was the first to cross the line. I thanked him for his gesture and asked what his time was. He had finished a solid minute slower than I would have, I felt a little better about being declared the winner.

As I have matured into a forty-something adult, I've worked very hard on switching over from "reacting" to "responding" to things I experience in my life. My desire to "give those race organizers a piece of my mind" was a reaction. The time I had over the last mile to drink in the details around me, and remember the bigger picture reason for the race, gave me the space and perspective to craft a response. It was just a race.

Our lives move pretty fast, and human nature typically drives us to react quickly to the things around us. We all need to find a way to take that extra mile, to think about our reactions and mold them into responses. When you do, you might not be the first across the line, but you just might go home with the top prize anyway.

We all feel the regret of reacting poorly to something, when a well-reasoned response would have been a better choice.

In the next week, as you feel yourself reacting to a situation, stop and take a moment to think things through. The persona or the situation that sparked your reaction might in fact deserve it, but will that help the situation? Probably not.

Figure out how to give yourself the space and time to respond instead of react. Initially it might take a while, but eventually it will become second nature, and that will be a first-place win for everyone.

21 – TIP-A-PALOOZA

Two months after graduating from college in 1991, I got a dog. She was a half-beagle, half-sheltie named Sylvia. For the first six months we lived in my parents' house, but then Sylvia and I moved to a tiny apartment in New York City.

Not long after moving in, Sylvia started getting into the garbage. Whenever I would leave her alone in the apartment for more than an hour, I would come home to find my kitchen garbage strewn all over my living room (the kitchen was one wall of the living room).

I WOULD CLEAN UP THE MESS, SCOLD THE DOG, AND HOPE MY MESSAGE WOULD SINK IN – IT DID NOT.

In every other way Sylvia was a perfectly lovely dog, so I was at a bit of a loss about what I could do to curb this undesirable behavior.

A few weeks later Sylvia and I went to the vet to get her some shots. After the business of the visit was over, I asked the vet what I could do to get the dog to stop eating the garbage. She looked me straight in the eye and said, "nothing, you will never get the dog to stop doing that."

I was both surprised and disappointed with her answer because Sylvia was only nine months old, and as far as I was concerned, she was still capable of learning a great deal. Furthermore, I was really getting sick of the clean-up routine.

After seeing the dejected look on my face, she went on: "the problem is that no matter how negative your reaction, she will always have the positive reinforcement of what she gets from the garbage; which is of course food. To a dog food is everything, so in your absence she will always be willing to take the chance that you'll be mad just to get the food. So, Steve you're not going to train the dog not to do that, you just need to make the garbage inaccessible."

The problem I was trying to solve (getting the dog to stop) was unsolvable. The solution was to accept the idea that the dog will always try to get at the garbage, and to simply make it impossible for her to get it.

Sylvia in her later years snuggling with an infant Oliver

The next day I bought a metal, flip-top garbage can with a latch that I could secure when leaving the house. A few times in the week following I found the garbage can knocked over, but the latch held. After that it was never a problem again.

I have shared with you before, that my wife and I have four children, one girl and three boys. When we moved into our current house, we only had two, with the third on the way. Not too long after, number four came along and our kitchen table was simply too small for the six of us.

It took several months, but I built us a new kitchen table, made of solid oak. In its smallest form it measures four feet wide and six feet long. It can be extended via two leaves an additional four feet to make a giant four by ten-foot table.

ONCE THE KIDS WERE ALL OUT OF HIGH CHAIRS AND YOUTH CHAIRS, WE NOTICED TWO PROBLEMS.

Whenever we had other people over (even a few) we had to get the extension leaves out because we couldn't fit an extra chair on either side of the table.

The larger problem was the tipping. There was some magical combination of my table design coupled with the geometry of our chairs that produced the ideal environment for child chair-tipping. Now, I recognize that with three boys, this was likely to be a bit of a problem no matter what, but what we were experiencing was epic. At any given moment, at least two, and often all four of them were tipping their chairs.

Foolishly, we thought somehow we could train, teach and otherwise discipline ourselves out of the tipping problem. So, with that in mind we set our sights on solving the seating flexibility problem.

After a bit of research I purchased two, six-foot long, unfinished solid wood benches. They arrived and were even heavier and sturdier than I had hoped. I finished them to match the table and we had solved our flexible seating problem. Normally two kids would sit on each bench, but we found that we could squeeze as many as five children on a side, making the standard set up of the table capable of seating twelve people, so long as they were small people.

A few days after installing the benches though, we noticed a funny thing – no tipping. Very much like the dog and the garbage, I don't think we ever would have been able to "legislate" our way through the tipping problem. So instead of making chair-tipping illegal, we made it irrelevant. Not only is it difficult to tip a bench, it isn't any fun because there is no back to push against. Furthermore, when you put another kid or two on the bench (who aren't interested in tipping) it makes tipping all but impossible.

Our kitchen table, benches and all

Every day we face problems that need addressing but all too often we let linear thinking take over, resulting in little or no progress. The best way to look at a situation before attempting a solution is to break it down as completely as you can. The answer is in there, but not always obvious, and most of the time it isn't your first instinct. This is one time I'm going to tell you to ignore your gut.

Cancer researchers have had good luck with this thinking. For the longest time their emphasis was "kill the tumor," but then they learned that you could more easily starve it in any number of ways. You don't have to kill something that is dying on its own, right?

So, the next time you're faced with something you can't quite solve, take a piece of paper and diagram all of the inputs, outputs, influences and related factors. Look at it long and hard and ask yourself; how can I change the equation to achieve the result I'm looking for?

The best part is, if you do it right (like we lucked out doing with the benches) the people (or dogs) being guided to change, won't even notice what's happening. I have yet to hear one of my kids say: "hey, we can't tip anymore!" Of course every once in a while they end up in one of the grown-up chairs at the end of the table, and you guessed it, TIP-A-PALOOZA!

What challenges do you face that seem intractable? Do you keep trying the same things with little or no progress?

Find a problem, just one, that has until now remained unsolved in your life. Write down the name of the problem in the middle of a piece of paper and start "diagramming" it. Identify all the inputs, outputs, variables and all the things that surround the problem. If you can identify something upstream that might make the problem disappear (or even impossible), you'll be on your way to success. When a problem refuses to respond to solution, throw out the solution and find a new one. If another approach isn't clear, change something in the equation (like we did with the benches) and it just might shed some light on what you're missing.

22 – CANINE HARDWARE & SOFTWARE

Way back in the 1970s, my dad came home from his pediatric practice one night and told us all about the computer they were about to buy for the office. It was an IBM System 34 minicomputer they planned to use for accounting and billing.

As my Dad was explaining the different parts of the computer and what each did, I had a lot of questions. He answered each one as best he could, but one statement he made is as clear to me today as it was nearly forty years ago:

"The parts of the computer that don't change, the cases, the electronics, all the stuff that hums, lights up and moves – that's called hardware. The instructions, the commands, the information it processes – that's called software because it can be changed, it's still 'soft'."

Keep in mind that a computer in the home (at least our home) was still more than a decade away, so as a society we were all learning the most basic terms that we all take for granted today.

The idea that the difference between hardware and software is the ability to change, applies to more than computers, but in these other areas, things aren't quite so black and white.

Back in the 1990s, I had a coworker named Bernard. He and his wife had a dog named Benny. The three of them lived in a cozy little house one town over from where I lived, and one weekend they invited me over for dinner.

At some point in the evening I asked to use the bathroom and as I walked down the hall, I observed something curious. In the middle of the main hallway of the house was something called a floor furnace. If you've never seen one, it is basically a small furnace that has no complex ductwork and it is installed in the floor in the middle of a small house. This one was about two feet wide by three feet long and what you saw was a metal grate that was flush with the floor.

As I walked toward the grate in the floor, Benny the dog was walking toward me in the opposite direction. I stepped onto the grate, but Benny made a purposeful change in course, and walked along the six-inch strip of floor between the grate and the wall. I asked Bernard about it and he said that Benny never walked on the grate and always went around.

A floor furnace installed in a hallway

THEY HAD EVEN PUT A DOG TREAT IN THE MIDDLE OF THE GRATE ONCE BUT BENNY WANTED NO PART OF IT.

Several years later, long after I had moved on to a new job, I ran into Bernard at the grocery store. After exchanging pleasantries he told me how he and his wife had just finished a major renovation and addition to their house. One of the things they had put in was a brand new heating and cooling system, so of course I had to ask,

"Do you still have the floor furnace?"

He said that they had taken it out and put brand new hardwood flooring in that hallway, but that Benny still only used the six-inches along the wall. They had even raised the challenge and put a piece of raw meat in the middle of the area that once held the metal grate. Benny opted to stay within his comfort zone.

Where Benny should have had software, he had hardware. Whatever unpleasant experience he had encountered with that floor furnace grate was so significant, that he was unwilling to risk ever stepping in that place again, even after the threat was clearly gone.

In the summer of 2014 I took on a project I had been ignoring for years. On the back of our house we have a lovely, three-sided screen porch. When the previous owners of the house had vinyl siding put on, they covered over the trim on the outside of the porch. The job was well done, and was such that the trim would never require painting. However, what they chose to do also made it impossible to replace any of the screens. At the time I took on this project, we had lived in the house for twelve years with four children and a dog named Nellie.

WERE THERE HOLES IN THE SCREENS? YOU BET THERE WERE.

Over the years I have patched and repaired the screens via a variety of methods, but this spring it became clear that a wholesale change was necessary.

So, with the help of my handy son Oliver, I started the process of removing all the trim, fixing the screens and installing all new trim in such a way that screens can be easily repaired.

Our porch with new screens and (not yet stained) new trim

One of the things I decided to do was relocate the dog door. The previous location was on the opposite corner of the porch from the door to the house, which caused the dog to track the maximum amount of dirt and snow across the carpet, all winter long. My plan was to move it much closer to the house, on the opposite side, right in line with an existing sidewalk.

As Oliver and I were working, there was a point where all the screens had been removed. I noticed as Nellie came and went, that she used the location of the old dog door, despite the fact that she could have walked "through the wall" anywhere.

I immediately thought of Benny and hoped Nellie would be a little more flexible.

A few hours later the new screens were up and the new dog door installed. Nellie came bounding out to the porch and headed straight for the location of the old dog door. From our positions outside, both Oliver and I shouted for her to stop.

ONE WINTER HER OLD DOG DOOR FROZE SHUT, AND WITHOUT HESITATION SHE MADE HER OWN POINT OF EGRESS RIGHT THROUGH A SCREEN. WE KNEW WHAT SHE WAS CAPABLE OF.

We rushed inside and showed her the new dog door, but she was not impressed.

Over the next few days we shoved her through the new door, and coaxed her with both treats, and her stuffed beaver toy named "Justin." At first the situation didn't look promising, Nellie kept going back to the old location, and would just stand there looking like some kind of sad doggie prisoner.

After a few days however, she started to get it.

I do worry about the next time she sees a squirrel or another dog, and simply runs without thinking, but I am hopeful that the "thinking" behavior she has learned will eventually become her default.

Nellie's new point of egress

I saw this phrase on Facebook one day and I think it applies here.

> ***BEFORE IT'S YOUR FAVORITE PLACE,***
> ***IT'S A PLACE YOU'VE NEVER BEEN.***

We all have our habits and our comfort zones, but when change and new opportunities lie before us we as humans have a choice: we can either be a Benny or a Nellie. Which one will you be?

Do you spend time outside your comfort zone? You should.

Pick something you do every day: the route you take to work, where you get your coffee, what radio station you listen to, or something similar. Now, force yourself to do that thing differently for the next seven days.

On day eight, you may decide to go right back to your old ways and that's fine, but at the very least you will be better off for the experience.

Stephen S. Nazarian

23 – SURVIVAL SKILLS

When you are in the Boy Scouts and you spend a lot of time preparing for both weekend, and weeklong camping trips, the conversations often turn to topics of survival. The scenarios conjured up are absurd.

Boys end up asking crazy questions of their leaders about days in the desert, or weeks on a mountaintop, and the best yet, months at sea in a life raft. As most people know, the limiting item in all survival situations is water. So boys being boys, the conversation eventually gets to the ultimate survival question:

SHOULD YOU DRINK YOUR OWN PEE?

Of course anyone with the smallest collection of survival skills will tell you: *absolutely not!* You should collect your urine and spread it on your skin in the heat of the day to keep your body from sweating as much. The evaporative cooling effect far outweighs any water you would get from drinking it. What's more, drinking pee would be nasty; I assume.

While none of my scout-mates nor I ever found ourselves in such a situation, it is good to know as much as you can, about what you can use in a pinch, when you don't have everything you think you need.

In the 2000 movie *Castaway*, the character played by Tom Hanks is marooned on an island, giving him no choice but to make due with what he has. At one point some FedEx boxes wash ashore. One of the boxes contains a pair of ice skates – useless right? Wrong, our protagonist used them to make a hatchet that eventually helps him build the raft that gets him off the island. In a pinch, he used what he had to accomplish what he needed to.

In 1968, my parents were stationed at Fort Leonard Wood Army Base in Waynesville, Missouri. I was born on the 12th day of December that year, and about a week later; my maternal grandparents came to visit from Pennsylvania.

It was a Christmas tradition in my mother's family to make a Swedish sausage called korv. My grandparents had brought with them their

Kitchenaid mixer, and the grinder/sausage attachment with which they intended to make the Viking-esque meat treat.

When sausage-stuffing time came, they set everything up in the kitchen, but there was a problem. The stuffing "tube" was missing, presumably still back in PA. Although just one of many parts involved in the process, the stuffing tube is absolutely critical. It is basically a meat funnel that squeezes the mushy mixture into the sausage casing. Trying to get by without it would be like trying to fill a 2-liter bottle by pouring liquid out of a 50-gallon drum – without spilling anything. It simply wouldn't be possible.

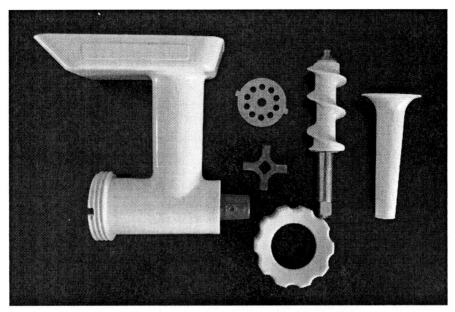

All parts of the sausage apparatus – the piece on the right was missing

Not wanting to disappoint their Swedish ladies, my father and grandfather set out into the Missouri wilderness on Christmas Eve in search of a solution. After visiting several stores of many kinds, they came home with a plastic funnel from an auto parts store, that after substantial modification, was made to fit into the Kitchenaid contraption and the sausage was made. The process was not as easy as it might have been, but they made due with what they had, and the goal was achieved.

FAST-FORWARD TWENTY-TWO YEARS AND ONE MONTH.

In my senior year of college at Lehigh University, I was a Resident Assistant (RA) in a dorm of 350 freshmen. After Christmas break, we were asked to return a few days ahead of the other students to get the dorm ready and to partake in some in-service training.

One night, all the RAs from my building were sitting around in the Assistant Hall Director's room. We were sharing stories from our respective holiday festivities while enjoying a variety of adult beverages.

The majority of us were seniors, but there were a few sophomores and juniors in the mix. One of the sophomores was always of the mind that he needed to prove himself in the presence of his older RA-mates, and most of the time his behavior reflected this attitude.

Dravo House - where Lehigh University keeps 350 freshmen every year

As the evening wore on, this sophomore made a significant effort to "talk smack" about all the things he would or could do, as well as, or better than the older folks in the room.

AFTER A WHILE SOMETHING HAD TO BE DONE.

We had a bottle of tequila and a whole package of disposable shot glasses. I looked straight into the sophomore's beady little eyes and said, "five tequila shots, right now, you and me."

IT WAS AT THIS POINT HE GAVE ME AN INCREDIBLE GIFT.

He leaned in towards me saying, "I'll wipe the floor with you, but first I have to go to the bathroom." As he rose and lumbered out of the room, I turned to the guy whose room we were in, and asked if he had any apple juice. You see, as a theatre major I had learned that even close-up apple juice looks just like scotch or tequila in the right glass.

A large smile grew across his face as he leaned over to his little dorm fridge, and retrieved a bottle of nicely chilled apple juice. We quickly poured five tequila shots for the precocious sophomore, while at the same time pouring me the same, but of apple juice.

WE BARELY GOT AWAY WITH IT.

As he returned from the bathroom, we just slid the apple juice back into the fridge. He sat down, looked at the shots before him, looked across the table at me and said something sophomoric, just as you might expect.

I finished all five of my shots in about four seconds and he struggled to get his down in half a minute. He admitted defeat and not long after, the evening broke up and we quietly went back to our respective rooms.

The next day in the cafeteria, I could see from across the room that "Mr. Tequila" didn't look so good. I filled my tray with food and then five little cafeteria glasses with apple juice. I sat down right across from him and said "boy am I thirsty." I proceeded to drink all five glasses in rapid succession right in front of him. It took a few minutes to sink in, but eventually he figured it out and he never talked smack again; at least not to me.

I challenge you to get creative to fix situations you face with what you have available. Before you know it you'll be enjoying Swedish sausage and apple juice, relaxing by the fire made of ice skate chopped wood. Your sense of accomplishment will provide you with the greatest pleasure of all, and you can skip pouring pee all over yourself; that's disgusting.

Look around and find something broken or identify a thing you need. The easy answer is to swap out the broken part or obtain exactly the thing you lack, but this week will be different. Fix the thing or solve the problem with only things you have already. No trips to Home Depot or Target allowed!

You'll soon get comfortable with the idea that there are multiple answers to every question and that the "right" way to do something can only be defined by you.

---

24 – WHEN IS A DUCK, NOT A DUCK?

Have you ever returned to a place you haven't been since you were a child? I think we've all had the experience of driving up to one of those places that exist so vividly in our minds, only to discover that the experience of time, combined with the growth of our bodies has taken this giant place from our past and shrunk it like a cotton sweater in a clothes dryer. "I remember it being bigger," has been uttered as long as people have been returning to the places of their youth.

I SUPPOSE IT IS ALL A MATTER OF PERSPECTIVE.

When you're little everything looks big, but your brain does a funny thing with both size, and the idea of size. My Father is five-eleven. Some time around the tenth grade he and I were the same height, but I continued growing to the six-foot-two that I am today. However, because my Dad was taller, and in charge for the first fifteen years of my life, in my mind I always see him as taller.

TO THIS DAY, THIRTY YEARS LATER, WHEN I THINK OF MY DAD, I THINK OF HIM AS TALLER.

There is a thing that geese and ducks do called imprinting. It is a pretty simple concept really. A baby goose or duck basically accepts the first thing that acts like a parent to it – as its parent.

It also accepts that it is a baby [insert thing] rather than being hard wired to be a goose or duck. So if a baby duck does not encounter a mother duck, but rather a basset hound. Once the basset hound treats the duck with love and compassion, the duck assumes the basset hound is its mother, AND that it is not a baby duck, but rather a baby basset hound.

This can happen very quickly and is not reversible. Once the imprint has been made, it is permanent. The effect is so strong that if the aforementioned duck were lost in a park and was given the choice to waddle towards a group of ducks or a group of basset hounds, it would choose the dogs. It sees the other ducks as different creatures than itself.

This is why when you see baby bird in captivity they are fed with bird-like puppets, not human hands.

When I was in my twenties, I was having a conversation with friend of my Dad's. We were talking about what a different experience it is to participate in kid activities, like going to an amusement park, as an adult. At some point in the conversation he said,

"HERE'S AN IDEA, WHAT IF WE BUILT AN ENTIRE AMUSEMENT PARK BUT WE MAKE EVERYTHING 30% BIGGER THAN NORMAL, THAT WAY GROWN-UPS CAN FEEL LIKE KIDS AGAIN."

We tossed the idea around a bit, and had some fun joking about how some shorter people we know wouldn't be able to ride the best rides, but in the end we decided that once the innocence of youth is lost, you couldn't bring it back with something as simple as a giant-sized tilt-o-whirl. It didn't sound nostalgic, it sounded creepy.

Late one spring I was with my three boys at little league opening day. My middle boy Oliver was with his team, so I was milling around with Lewis and Lawrence as the opening ceremonies took place. They were seven and five respectively at the time.

When I played little league, the umpires held a giant blue pad in front of their chest to protect themselves from wayward pitches.

Since then, they have developed pads umps wear under their shirts. Some pads are smaller than others, but as we stood watching the endless speeches by politicians and the little league board, an umpire was approaching Lawrence and me.

Umpire chest protectors as I remember them

This particular ump was probably six-four with a shaved head and sporty sunglasses. He was wearing one of the thicker under-the-shirt pads. As he walked passed us, Lawrence tugged at my shirt. I bent down to hear what he had to say and as I did, he pointed at the ump and said,

"DAD, LOOK, A SUPERHERO."

He had taken several data points and come to a logical conclusion that only a five-year-old could. A very tall man with a shiny head, cool sunglasses, and an unnaturally large torso could only be one thing – a superhero.

It has been said many times that youth is wasted on the young and in a way that is true, but at the same time not. Only after we have grown out of the magic, innocence and wonder of youth do we long for it once again. You truly can't appreciate it until you've lost it.

It has also been said:

IF A MAN SAYS YOU'RE UGLY, HE'S MEAN.
IF A WOMAN SAYS YOU'RE UGLY, SHE'S JEALOUS.
IF A LITTLE KID SAYS YOU'RE UGLY, YOU'RE UGLY.

Kids have the benefit of not yet being hardened. They have not yet been "imprinted" by the world around them, and because of this they are free to be completely honest and transparent.

Fortunately, even though we as adults have lost much of our youthful pliability and openness, we have more capacity for elasticity than the imprinted duckling or gosling. We may be less flexible than before, but we do have the ability to recognize it and adapt to it.

I'm reminded of that scene in the movie *BIG* where Tom Hanks' character Josh is sitting in a toy design meeting in the company where he works. All the smart adults presented their ideas for a new toy and the dialogue goes like this:

Josh: It turns from a building into a robot, right?

Paul: Precisely.

Josh: Well, what's fun about that?

Paul: Well, if you had read your industry breakdown, you would see that our success in the action figure area has climbed from 27 percent to 45 percent in the last two years. There, that might help.

Josh is simply being honest about the toy not sounding fun (which is what kids do) and Paul, the grown-up is hiding behind his data (which is what grown-ups do). The beautiful thing about the scene is that unlike an imprinted duck, the grown-ups in the room start to listen to the kid and eventually see things his way.

As we grow, mature and take on responsibilities, we stop thinking with our heart and gut, and instead make decisions based on data and best practices. It is definitely safer, but it will never be the source of brilliance.

Thank goodness we don't harden as quickly as the gosling or duckling. We humans have the ability to go back and think like a kid, and we should as often as we can.

Sure we can temper impulsive thoughts with data and experience, but we should lead with our heart and trust our gut. If we don't we're nothing more than a duck that thinks it is a basset hound.

For the next seven days, take every opportunity you can to think like a kid. If you get stuck, ask a kid, they will always give you a completely honest answer.

You will encounter resistance, but keep the faith. When someone tells you your approach lacks sufficient data to be reasonable, reply with a kid-like answer. I'm not suggesting you call your co-worker a "dooty-head" but rather infuse your defense with awe, joy and wonder. You just might get those grown-ups to come around after all.

---

25 – RECURSION

When I was maybe ten years old my Dad took me to the Albright-Knox Art Gallery in Buffalo, NY. One of the pieces on exhibit was something called Room No. 2, but everyone just called it The Mirror Room.

I remember having to take off my shoes to go inside, but once I did, I was consumed with the images that came from mirrors in every direction. At the time I had no idea what the effect was called, but I did know that it was way cool. Unlike a carnival "House of Mirrors" which is designed to distort and confuse, this piece was made up of perfectly flat mirrors placed either perfectly parallel or perpendicular to each other.

No matter where I looked there were thousands of "Steves" disappearing into the depths of the mirrors. I do not recall what I was wearing, but it was the 1970s, so we can assume it was something truly awful.

Interior decorators call two mirrors in parallel planes an "infinity mirror" but as I learned in eighth grade math, what I experienced standing in

Room No. 2

my striped tube socks, in a Buffalo art gallery, was something called recursion.

I LOVE RECURSION.

My elementary school was not normal. Every room was shaped like a hexagon and there were no walls between the classrooms. I am not making this up.

Like every elementary school in America, we received a flyer several times a year giving us the opportunity to buy books through the Scholastic Corporation.

For years my mom was the coordinator for this program. Despite the difficulty of making sense of orders placed by grade school children using stubby pencils, wads of crumpled singles, and ratty brown bags filled with pennies and nickels; she always made it work and the result was that thousands of books were delivered to, and read by, my fellow schoolmates. Thanks mom!

One of the things you could order from the Scholastic book company was the Dynamite Magazine. For the elementary school crowd of the 1970s, this was People Magazine, TMZ and Perez Hilton all rolled up into one. If you didn't read Dynamite, you did not know what was "goin' on."

At about the same time, there was a sitcom on television called *Good Times* that starred a comedian named Jimmie Walker. The character he played was named J.J. Evans. J.J. was an exuberant, happy character whose catch phrase was a loud utterance of the word "DY-NO-MITE!"

The April 1975 issue of Dynamite magazine, featured Jimmie Walker on the cover holding a copy of Dynamite magazine, featuring Jimmie Walker on the cover holding a copy of Dynamite magazine, featuring Jimmie Walker... well you get the idea.

The most recursive cover of the 1970s

At the time I knew it was cool, but looking at it today reveals so many layers of recursion that if I stare at it too long, I fear it may in fact blow my mind.

In spring 2014, I stumbled across an item (I am reluctant to call it a story) where the actor Ryan Gosling was photographed wearing a t-shirt bearing an image of actor Macaulay Culkin on the cover of Life Magazine. Not to be outdone, Mr. Culkin had a shirt made of the image of Mr. Gosling wearing the shirt of Mr. Culkin.

Art imitating life - imitating art - recursion is everywhere

Of course this is where the Internet and Photoshop take over. I have no idea how much of this is real and how much is BS, but as a lover of recursion I think this is absolutely fabulous.

So why am I writing about my love of recursion? Well, as you read in the introduction of this book, most of the chapters were originally posts on my blog about creative problem solving. Early one morning I sat down to look at the board where I keep the post-it notes of my ideas, and none of them looked good to me.

I went downstairs to get a cup of coffee and I started to think about writing a blog post about the act of writing a blog post. The firing off of ideas in my head went something like this:

I should write about writing. Oh, that's recursive – I love recursion. What about that mirror room in that museum in Buffalo? Ooh, ooh, what about that cover of Dynamite magazine with Jimmie Walker?

Oh man, that's just like that Macaulay Culkin, Ryan Gosling thing I saw last week – I guess I have something to write about now, I sure hope I can find an image of that magazine cover from the 1970s.

Of course this all took place in my brain on the 45-second walk from the coffee machine to my desk.

THIS IS IN FACT WHAT IT IS LIKE TO BE INSIDE MY BRAIN; PRETTY MUCH ALL THE TIME.

So often we only look only outward for the solutions we need. We ask others, we go buy stuff, we dig deep into books and the Internet seeking the information that will satisfy the need of the moment. The television show the X-files proclaimed in every episode:

"THE TRUTH IS OUT THERE."

I put it to you today that the truth (or the data, or the idea, or the answer) you seek may not be out there, but in fact be inside you already. Practice a little personal recursion and I think you'll be pleased with what you find. The morning I wrote this, my discovery was DY-NO-MITE!

I have previously challenged you to fix something or solve a problem with resources you had lying around. This week, instead of looking to other sources when you need information, look inward.

Find the place where you do your best thinking (or day dreaming), mowing the lawn, taking a bath, going for a run or something like that. Before starting the activity write down 2-3 things for which you need ideas and then let the Zen of your thinking happy-place do the work.

You have a thing in your head that is a lot like Pintrest, but instead of pictures of gluten-free bran muffins and glitter-covered craft projects, it is made of your experiences and memory. It is a way better resource than you've ever given it credit for. It's about time you gave it a try.

26 – TRUST BUT VERIFY

Ronald Reagan was famous for saying, that when handling a negotiation of any kind, he liked to: "Trust but verify."

I have used this philosophy in my business life, and as a parent. Think what you want about Ronald Regan, but it is hard to imagine the iron curtain falling under any other type of leadership in Washington.

When I worked for an IT consulting firm in Manhattan in the 1990s, the owners decided that the company needed an image overhaul. The company was called Galaxy Systems and their brochure (this was before most companies had websites) was a simple tri-fold with a picture on the front of; well, a galaxy. It was as ugly as it was literal.

A client introduced us to a fancy Manhattan "Branding Agency" who came in to talk to us about our plans. Basically we needed a new logo and all the things that go with it: letterhead & envelopes, a company color palate, some standard fonts and a simple style guide.

After a one-hour meeting, they said they would be back in a few days with their proposal. When they returned their plan was simple:

WE PAY THEM $15,000 AND THEY WOULD GIVE US OUR NEW LOGO; ONE DESIGN, NO EDITS.

They were very confidant in their abilities to, as they put it, "hit a home run on the first pitch." We were not pleased with this approach and when we said as much, their confidence turned into insolence, and they basically stormed off in a huff.

THEY WANTED US TO TRUST, BUT WITH NO PROVISION FOR VERIFYING. WE WENT WITH ANOTHER COMPANY.

At around the same time, I was enjoying living in my very first house. It was a super "fixer-upper" and I spent my evenings and weekends transforming it from a shack, into a slightly nicer shack.

Coming home to a stuffy house a several warm summer days in a row, I decided to open the top sash of a few windows while I was at work to see if that would help. There were no screens on the upper sashes, but I figured I could handle a few bugs. When I returned home that night, the house was much less stuffy.

I WENT ABOUT MY NORMAL EVENING ACTIVITIES.

Around eleven, I put my dogs to bed in the laundry room, locked the doors, shut out the lights and went into my bedroom to watch TV before going to sleep. As I sat on my bed watching a Law & Order rerun, I decided I wanted a beer, so without turning on any lights, I crossed the living room towards the fridge.

AS I RETURNED THROUGH THE DARK ROOM, COLD BEER IN HAND, SOMETHING FLEW BY MY HEAD

I was so startled I dropped to the ground. I scooted over to the wall and flipped on the lights, but I saw nothing. I grabbed a flashlight and looked in all the corners of the large living room with the vaulted ceiling, but whatever had just "buzzed the tower" was nowhere to be seen.

I decided to recreate the previous conditions. I turned off all the lights and sat quietly in the corner of the room, flashlight at the ready. It only took a few minutes before I heard the soft sound of fluttering wings again and as I flipped on the flashlight I confirmed my worst fear – a bat.

THERE WAS A BAT IN MY HOUSE AND I HAD NO IDEA WHAT TO DO ABOUT IT.

I confirmed that if I turned the lights on it would hide, so I did what any rational person would do. I turned on all the lights in the living room, grabbed my beer, closed my bedroom door and figured there was nothing I could do until morning.

The next morning was bright and sunny, so I was fairly certain that my flying mammalian friend was going to stay put. I cracked open the yellow pages under Pest Control and picked a company the next town over. Their ad specifically mentioned bats. It was only 7:30 but the yellow page listing clearly stated "24 Hour Service," their words, not mine.

After about twenty rings, a groggy man answered. I introduced myself, explained my situation and he listened without interruption. After a long pause and rather unpleasant "I just got up and haven't yet had a cigarette" cough, he stated his position:

"Ok Steve here's the deal. Bats are tricky. I can come over there and try and flush it out and try to catch it. If that doesn't work I can set some traps. If those don't work I can put out some poisoned food, but then if it hides and dies you've got a dead bat rotting somewhere in your house. Minimum to come try and catch a bat, $450 and we go from there."

I took all of this in and replied, "so what you're basically telling me is that for $450 you can come to my house and maybe catch the bat. But, if you can't, you keep the $450 and I still have a bat in my house."

SENSING MY SKEPTICISM HE SAID, "SO, DO YOU WANT ME TO COME OUT?"

I politely declined, got dressed and went to work. The Internet was new and (I know this is hard to believe) when you did a search for information you often found nothing. This is what happened when I started doing bat research on my office computer. Since my office was only a few blocks from the main branch of the New York Public Library, (or as many know it, the "Ghostbusters Library") I popped over there on my lunch hour to see what I could find.

Stone lions guard the knowledge at the New York Public Library

I looked up everything I could about what kinds of bats were native to my area, how they behaved, what they like to eat, and I even managed to find a few tips on how to catch them.

When I got home that night I had a plan. I placed my 8-foot stepladder in the middle of the living room. On the top of it I placed a blob of peanut butter, a small dish of water and half of an over-ripe peach that I had purchased specifically for this task.

I made a net by straightening the hook of a wire hangar, and duct taped it to the end of a broom handle. I then pulled the triangle of the hangar into a circle and taped a plastic grocery bag around the perimeter.

AS THE SUN WENT DOWN, I SAT IN THE CORNER OF MY LIVING ROOM AND WAITED.

Not too long after it got dark, it started to rain. It wasn't a light drizzle either, this was heavy, roof-tapping rain, so when the bat started to fly around my living room I didn't hear it at first. When I clicked on the flashlight to check my "bait ladder" there it was perched on the edge of the top step, face full of juicy peach – gotcha you airborne rat!

I slowly rose and started to walk toward the ladder, but he was having none of that and immediately took to the air. He flew around the living room, but it didn't take me long to notice that he was flying in a somewhat repeating pattern. I sat still studying him for about a minute and then put my net where I expected him to be next. Bingo!

I had the bat in the net, but it wasn't over yet. Using my very best lacrosse cradling skills (of which I have none) I kept the bat in the back of my makeshift net until I was able to walk out my front door.

It was still raining rather hard, so I simply flung the entire net, broom, bat combo into my front yard and slammed the door. The next morning the bat was gone.

There was a great commercial for UPS a few years ago where a couple of consultants are shown making a list of recommendations to a client. When the client says, "let's do it" the consultants get uncomfortable and begin to laugh, because they don't do, they just recommend.

Certainly my company needed a new logo, but we weren't willing to bet fifteen-large on the ego of a single company.

I had a bat in my house, but the supposed "expert" on the other end of the phone wanted $450 to come over and "try" to remove it.

There are lots of folks out there who will happily take your money to try and solve a problem, but in the end if they want your trust and are unwilling to offer you the chance to verify, walk away. All they are selling is the idea that they have a greater comfort level in trying than you do.

$450 for trying? Hell, we can all try anything ourselves – for free.

Is it killing you to spend money hiring people that you know aren't nearly as smart or clever as you know yourself to be? Expertise without a guarantee is nothing but false bravado.

This is the week when you ignore the so-called experts and take on a challenge that most people would say you're crazy to try. I don't care what it is, just start.

The best part is that the Internet (especially YouTube) is full of advice and information to help you not screw it up (too much).

You will make mistakes and you will make a mess, but when you succeed I expect you to shout about it from the rooftops. Get on social media, post pictures and tell the world "I fought the system and the system lost!"

Trusting in yourself (and verifying it with results) is one of the greatest feelings in the world.

Stephen S. Nazarian

27 – ONLY IF THEY LOVE YOU

My wife Emily is an ICU Pediatrician. The work she and her colleagues do is incredibly important, but at the same time very stressful. She and I were married just as she began her formal training for this particular sub-specialty, and almost immediately I noticed something.

This group of doctors, nurses and other professionals who deal with exceptionally complex medicine, and life/death issues daily; function much more like a family than a group of coworkers.

At first, my observations with how they treated each other had me thinking that they were either dysfunctional or crazy, but once I looked at it all through the lens of a family, it all made complete sense. What they face, and how they deal with it, requires a level of honesty, exposure and familiarity normally reserved for brothers and sisters.

INTENSIVE CARE PHYSICIANS ARE NOT COWORKERS – THEY ARE FAMILY.

This is why one of their common forms of expression is that of the complex practical joke. Since you can only get away with embarrassing and abusing those who have no choice but to love you, the complex practical joke is only appropriate for those tied by blood, not just a job.

In the early 1970s, we used to travel several times a year, to visit my Mother's parents in Bradford, PA. My mother was the only child in the Carlson family, and as such had unilateral responsibility for her parents.

My Grandmother, Eleanor, was an intense woman. Being of 100% Swedish extraction, she wielded her feelings and opinions in a stoic, but severe way that only a race of people who spend three months a year in total darkness can.

My Grandfather Dick, on the other hand, was a gregarious and affable guy whose outgoing and caring ways caused him to be well loved in every corner of his life. Being of the same cultural heritage as my Grandmother, he was a bit of an anathema to his roots.

WHERE MY GRANDMA WAS MOSTLY INGMAR BERGMAN AND VOLVO, MY GRANDPA WAS ALL VIKING AND ABBA.

Since my mother was an only child, my father quickly became the son my Grandpa never had. And once my brother and I came along, he truly enjoyed hanging out with "the boys" when we would come to visit.

The pit of the incinerator with its claw, looked just like this one

Where they lived, there was no regular garbage collection. Every few days you would swing by "the dump" with your detritus, and toss it into the pit. "The dump" was a bit of a misnomer since it wasn't actually a dump. Though I suppose at one time it had been one; where you took your garbage by 1975 was instead a large incinerator.

It was set up for you to pull your car up to the loading dock, and fling your garbage thirty feet into the pit. Above the pit was an enormous mechanical claw that would pick up the garbage and place it into the hopper that led to the incinerator. A menacing sight for two young boys to be sure.

During a visit one warm summer Saturday morning, my Grandpa loaded up the trunk with refuse, my Dad rode shotgun, and my brother and I bounced around the back seat as we made the short drive to the dump.

Grandpa backed his butterscotch Chevy Nova up to the edge of the pit, and we all got out. My Father, eager to be helpful, quickly came around to the back and began moving the contents of the trunk into the pit. My grandpa let him do so.

As my father did the dirty work, the dump supervisor named "Trigger" came over to chat. My father made quick work of the bags and boxes and in one final motion; he leaned into the trunk, grabbed the last box (an old round cardboard hat box) and enthusiastically shot it far out into the pit.

MY GRANDPA LET OUT A GASP.

"What did you do that for?" he shrieked. The color drained from my Father's face (not common for an Armenian) and panicking he replied, "what did I do?" With a completely straight face Grandpa continued, "That was Eleanor's favorite box! You're supposed to toss what's inside, not the box itself. Man-o-man are you in trouble."

EVEN AT MY YOUNG AGE, I KNEW THAT YOU WANTED TO AVOID GETTING IN TROUBLE WITH GRANDMA CARLSON.

My Father looked out at the hatbox in the pit, then looked back at my Grandpa and Trigger, then looked at my brother and me, and then back out at the hatbox. "I'll climb down and get it, there's a ladder right over there." He pointed to the far corner of the pit.

Trigger, who up to now had said not a word, chimed in saying, "Well... that claw is automatic. I can't control it. When it wants to go, it goes."

MY BROTHER AND I LOST IT. "DAD, YOU CAN'T GO INTO THE PIT, THE CLAW'S GOING TO GET YOU!"

The debate went on for several minutes, with my father insisting he had to do something, and my brother and me wailing, picturing our dad being swallowed up by the claw. Grandpa and Trigger said nothing – until they burst out laughing. The whole thing had been a setup.

The hatbox was in fact garbage, and the only thing that needed saving was my father's pride. However, knowing the effort his father-in-law had gone through to pull off the trick, my father's feelings quickly turned from feeling duped, to feeling loved.

In the fall of 1999, my wife and I were visiting her parents in Virginia. We had only been married for six months, but I had already been warmly welcomed into her family. We arrived at my in-law's home late one morning. As we discussed our plans for the visit, my mother-in-law suggested that her husband and I go grocery shopping.

We got into the car and made the fifteen-minute drive to the Food Lion. We walked up and down the aisles, filling the cart with the items from the list, plus a few things that looked worth adding.

As we walked down the chip aisle, my father-in-law turned to me and asked, "do you like pork rinds?" I didn't really have an opinion either way, but wanting to be agreeable to the patriarch of my newly acquired family, I responded with a simple, "sure." He carefully placed two bags in the cart and we continued on, I didn't think a thing of it. We finished the list, checked out and loaded the bags into the trunk of the Crown Victoria.

We drove home, unloaded all the bags and brought them into the kitchen. My wife and mother-in-law were there to receive us, and they got right to putting things away. When my mother-in-law got to the two bags of pork rinds, she put her hands on her hips, looked right at my shopping partner and scolded, "Paul! Pork Rinds?!?"

WITHOUT BREAKING HIS CALM EXPRESSION, HE LOOKED RIGHT AT HER AND SAID, "STEVE WANTED THEM."

[Insert sound of new son-in-law being thrown under a bus.]

Was he using me to get his hands on some otherwise disallowed deep-fried-pork-fat? You bet he was, but I didn't mind because I knew that the very act of involving me in his skullduggery was a statement of love.

Our four children fight with each other at a level that sometimes baffles my wife and me. However, we also know that if push came to shove, that they would protect and defend each other with equal or even greater vigor. Family, blood or otherwise, is funny that way.

So if you occasionally fall victim to a well-planned practical joke, or crime of opportunity, remember that those who perpetrate such things will involve you... only if they love you.

After you get over the initial embarrassment, it is a pretty awesome feeling and one of the better initiation rituals of American society.

This week is going to be fun. Your job is simple, pick a victim, make a plan, and execute an amazing practical joke.

There is one rule; you can't be mean to anyone involved. Mild embarrassment is encouraged, but humiliation is to be avoided. Try and involve others that love your victim as much as you do. It will make it more fun and much easier to pull off. Be warned – your opening shot will likely inspire a response – but only if they love you.

---

28 – DRUNK UNCLE GLOW STICK

My daughter Charlotte is an entrepreneur. Sure, we all have ideas and thoughts of doing something big, but some people have a genetic predisposition to making things happen, and turning ideas into businesses. My daughter is one of those people.

Several years ago after tasting a cake-pop at Starbucks, she decided that they were delicious enough that everyone would want to have them, but they were also too expensive.

So, she did some research on how to make them, started experimenting and a few boxes of cake mix later, she had a process that worked. At first she just made them for fun and gave them away to family, friends and sent them to work with my wife.

A few months into this process my wife and I were headed to a neighborhood function where we were to bring a dessert. It was a brunch for the neighborhood football pool, so Charlotte asked if she could make football-shaped cake balls (that's what she calls them).

She did a nice job and as we were packing up to go, she came into the kitchen and said, "don't forget these." In her hand she had a stack of business cards that she strategically placed among the sugary little footballs.

Pretty soon orders started flowing in from folks in the neighborhood and my wife's coworkers. She even scored a multi-week contract with the booster club from a local high school. They sold basketball shaped cake balls at the concession stand for the entire varsity season.

LITTLE DID I KNOW SHE WAS JUST GETTING WARMED-UP.

Our house is adjacent to an elementary school. To the east, where our yard ends the schoolyard begins. At the other end of the schoolyard is a town park where the annual Fourth of July festivities take place. Our yard is therefore one of the very best places in town for watching fireworks.

The town puts on a pretty nice shindig in the park, but there is almost no parking. If you are one of the 20,000 plus people who come to "ooh-and-aah" at the fireworks, you have two choices: park in the plaza across the street from the park and be guaranteed an hour of traffic with cranky kids at 10:30pm, or you can park in my neighborhood and walk over.

The latter is a very popular choice. So much so that the town comes through on the 3rd of July and posts no-parking signs on one side of the street to keep things safe.

Satellite imagery of my neighborhood

Two doors down from our house is a sidewalk that connects the neighborhood to the schoolyard. This is the funnel through which hundreds (if not thousands) of people flow on their way from neighborhood parties and reasonable parking into, and out of the park festivities.

THERE IS A SAYING: "THE THREE MOST IMPORTANT THINGS TO CONSIDER WHEN OPENING A RETAIL ESTABLISHMENT ARE: LOCATION, LOCATION, AND LOCATION."

This location is almost too perfect – one day a year. Since my daughter is always on the lookout for opportunity, she seized on this one. The first thing she did was make a deal with the neighbor girl, whose yard is adjacent the sidewalk. Then she turned to me for financing. She wanted to sell:

- Cake balls & Popcorn
- Water
- Glow sticks
- Little American Flags

This was going to require a bit of an outlay. She needed $50. I offered her two options:

1. Make me a 50% partner and share the profits/loss equally

2. Pay me the $50 back, plus a $5 fee by the 5th of July - even if she lost money

**SHE'S NO FOOL. SHE KNEW SHE WAS SITTING ON A GOLDMINE.
SHE TOOK OPTION TWO.**

We got her set up with our 10' pop-up tent, a table and few strings of Christmas lights. She made cake balls, bought water, glow sticks, and flags and set up the popcorn popper. She was ready to sell by 5:00pm.

The first year she did this, she walked back to our house at 6:30, handed me my $55 and with raised eyebrows said "we good?" That year, after paying for all the supplies and tipping-out all her little helpers, she netted $85, but there was much room for improvement.

The cake balls were hard to keep from melting and they didn't sell well. She had a good half of them left over and they were too mushy to keep. That took a bite out of her profit. Popcorn was a loser. They only sold a few.

Water and glow sticks sold out, and way before she ran out of opportunity to sell them. What's worse, as she tried to push the cake balls after the fireworks were over, people just wanted to buy more glow sticks.

The next year, she decided to sell only glow sticks, flags and water. She figured she could stock up well beyond her sales expectations and return whatever she didn't sell, so long as the packages weren't opened.

**THIS TIME SHE ASKED FOR $100.
I ASKED FOR THE SAME 10% VIG.**

She nailed it. When the first firework went off, she still had inventory but had sold way more than she thought she would.

There is something that she calls the ***drunk uncle effect*** that was responsible for a good portion of the glow stick sales.

Basically if there is a group of kids accompanied by adults who have been enjoying adult beverages, the "fun uncle" of the group (biological or appointed) has a tendency to whip out a twenty or two and proclaim "GLOW STICKS FOR EVERYONE!"

Charlotte also sent one of her little helpers down into the park to benchmark water prices. Once she determined that the least expensive bottle in the park was $2, she set her price at $1.50 each or 4 for $5. Her sign simply read… "cheapest water you're going to see tonight."

**YEAR TWO NETTED HER NORTH OF $125,
FOR MY THEN TWELVE-YEAR-OLD DAUGHTER.**

The next year we were out of town for Independence Day, but each successive year she does her analysis and planning for another successful stand. She now pre-packages some glow sticks in $20 bundles to make it even easier for the "drunk uncles." She no longer needs me for financing.

Businesses (or any ideas) don't succeed overnight; they take time and require adaptation. Charlotte thought her idea would boost her cake ball business. But, by responding to the market, she became the Glow Stick Queen of Penfield Gardens, if only for one day a year. She still enjoys making cake balls, but she makes a whole pile more money keeping the patriotic throngs of Penfield hydrated and glowing.

If you have an idea, and a fear of failure is holding you back, take some comfort in knowing that nothing ever goes as planned. You will experience failure, but if you keep a keen eye on things, the opportunities that are bound to succeed will reveal themselves to you. Every business has its "drunk uncles." Go out and find yours.

What is holding you back; fear, lack of time, lack of resources, people telling you "it won't work?" The only way to prove something will or won't work is to do it.

This week is a big one – go out and start that thing you've been thinking about, but have been afraid to start.

IT WILL NOT GO AS PLANNED – but start it anyway.

Figure out what the big-picture goal is and focus on that; making all you moves and changes in support of that goal. Don't be too specific. Make you goal more like "sell things to neighbors & make money," not "grow my cake ball business."

Remember, I did not set out to write a book, yet here you are reading it. I can only help you with one word – start. The rest is up to you.

---

29 – BIG CONCERT, BIG RESPONSIBILITY

In the summer of 1985 they held a huge concert in both London and Philadelphia – it was called Live Aid. It was the first of the mega-star-studded events to raise money for a cause. This particular cause was food aid for Africa, but the artists and their performances were at least as significant as the altruism.

That summer I worked for an athletic shoe and clothing store in town called SneaKee Feet. The manager of the store was a guy named Ruben.

My actual nametag from SneaKee Feet

Ruben lived his life by his own set of rules and although some of his decisions were questionable, we didn't say anything because he was the boss.

The weekend that Live Aid took place; Ruben rented a VCR from a video shop one town over. He wanted to tape both concerts from start to finish so he would have them to play back – presumably some day when he owned a VCR of his own.

**BELIEVE ME WHEN I TELL YOU,
THIS ALL MADE COMPLETE SENSE IN THE 80'S.**

I walked into the store a few minutes before 9:00am for work the Monday after the concert, and Ruben immediately pulled me aside. The district manager was due at the store any minute and Ruben needed to return the VCR to the video shop by 10:00am or he'd be charged for another day. "Steve man, I need you to drive the VCR back to the store."

Normally this kind of request would be no problem, but there was a small issue. I only had a learner's permit. I told Ruben this, but he simply responded, "I don't care man, take my car and return the VCR."

So I did what the boss said. I took his keys and drove his car, a Renault 18i, out of the plaza and up the hill to the video store. Each way on the 1.5 mile journey, I was certain I would see one of my parents and be grounded forever. Of course, I was able to return the VCR without incident, and as they read these words, this is the first my parents are hearing of this. I sure hope the statute of limitations on "bad judgment" has run out.

NINE YEARS LATER...

In the summer of 1994, I was working for Crest Audio in Paramus, NJ and as I have noted in other stories, in the summer my job included attending several concerts a week.

At the time Lollapalooza was the biggest rock-n-roll festival touring the country. Lollapalooza 1994 was an all-day, multi-stage extravaganza with the headlining acts being the Beastie Boys and The Smashing Pumpkins. On August second, the tour came to Saratoga Springs, NY.

Along with our Sales Director Greg McVeigh, I was to travel to the hallowed grounds of the Saratoga Raceway, meet up with our customers, bring the roadies clean t-shirts, take pictures of our gear in use, and generally live a day of the proverbial "rock-n-roll lifestyle."

The day before we were going to the concert, my boss pulled me aside and asked if I would bring his sixteen-year-old son Merlin along for the day. Merlin was visiting the states for the summer, and in two weeks he was returning to England where he lived with his mother. Of course I said yes.

IT WAS A SIXTEEN-YEAR-OLD FOREIGNER AT AN ALL-DAY ROCK FESTIVAL. WHAT COULD POSSIBLY GO WRONG?

The next morning Greg and I picked up Merlin at 5:00am for the three-hour drive to the concert.

THE FIRST SIGN OF TROUBLE CAME WHEN WE TRIED TO PARK THE CAR.

If you're unfamiliar, the town of Saratoga Springs NY is famous for a few things:

- Natural mineral springs that claim to have healing powers
- The Saratoga horse-racing complex
- The Saratoga Performing Arts Center (SPAC)

Beyond that, it is a fancy little town about 40 miles north of Albany.

It is my understanding that the town lays out the red carpet for the horseracing crowd on the weekends, since they are both civilized and well heeled. These visitors are so welcome, that locals near the racetrack rent out their yards for parking. So when we pulled into a yard with a large sign saying "Parking $5," we thought we were all set, except August 2nd was a Tuesday.

As we were climbing out of our car, several other concert-going cars pulled into the yard alongside us. There were at least five cars unloading in the yard when an angry, elderly woman appeared on the front porch of the house and screamed, "get your dirty rock-n-roll cars out of my yard!" When Greg motioned toward the sign welcoming us for a fiver, she continued, "that parking is only for the horse crowd, not YOUR kind."

No mention of rock-n-roll

This is the pass you want at any concert

We moved the car to a spot on the street and headed into the concert. Waiting for us at will-call were all-access and photo passes for me and Greg, and a restricted access pass for Merlin. We bypassed the long lines and were quickly let in via the crew entrance. Things were looking up.

Once we were inside Merlin turned to me and Greg and said, "Listen mates, you don't want to babysit me and I don't want to get in the way of your work. What do you say we pick a time and place to meet up later and we can all go do our own thing?"

Greg and I looked at each other and then we looked back at Merlin. He was about 5' 10" and soaking wet he maybe weighed 120 pounds. He had bleached, white, spiky hair, and was wearing cargo shorts and a white t-shirt. He certainly looked the part. Greg and I looked at each other again, shrugged our shoulders and in unison said, "yeah, sure, why not."

As the son of a life-long professional audio guy, I assumed Merlin knew his way around a concert set-up. So I told him to meet us at the "Front Of House" position at 4:00pm.

For those who don't know, when anyone involved in concert sound says "Front Of House" (FOH) position, he is referring to that place where the sound engineer stands and twiddles all those colorful knobs on that giant mixing board.

> *MERLIN SMILED, SAID "THANKS MATES" AND DISAPPEARED INTO THE GROWING CROWD. IT WAS 8:30AM.*

Greg and I had a productive day meeting with customers, getting all kinds of equipment shots and meeting several of the artists. By the time 4:00pm rolled around we were tired, dirty, and ready to think about heading home. We had never planned to stay to the very end.

We arrived at the FOH at 3:55. The mosh-pit was in full writhe, right in front of us, so we used our all access passes to wait behind the protection of the FOH fence. By 4:15, Merlin had not yet arrived. By 4:25 we started to worry. At 4:35 we decided that Greg should stay put and I should go out to the car to see if I could find him.

> *REMEMBER, IT WAS 1994 – NOBODY HAD CELL PHONES.*

It turns out that when we had left him seven and a half hours earlier, Merlin was careful to note the name of meeting place, but had no idea what it meant. At 3:55 when he started asking people, such as the guy at the Häagen-Dazs cart, where the "front house" was, but he had no luck. So, after thirty minutes of being unable to find the elusive "front house" he gave up and headed back into town towards the car.

Merlin left the concert, walked several blocks through town, and when he found the car empty and locked, he decided to turn back. What he hadn't noticed was a small group of "townies" had taken an interest in this odd-looking kid. As he began his walk back to the concert, these boys emerged from between two houses surrounding young Merlin.

I can only assume they were closely related to the aforementioned "angry grandma" and as such has little tolerance for "our kind." They taunted Merlin with questions and once they heard his British accent… well, that was it.

> *THEY GAVE THE BOY A GOOD OLD-FASHIONED REDNECK BEAT DOWN, AND THEN THEY SCURRIED BACK INTO WHATEVER HOLE FROM WHICH THEY HAD EMERGED.*

When I finally found poor Merlin limping towards the festival gates, his shirt was torn and bloody, and his face was a bit, well, lopsided. I had a security guard radio over to the FOH and told Greg to meet us at the car. We got some dinner, and cleaned up Merlin as best we could before making the three-hour drive home.

It was around 9:00pm when we pulled into the driveway to return Merlin to his dad, my boss. Fortunately, his reaction was predominantly one of sympathy, and the fears of job loss I had been wrestling with for hours were unfounded.

In both of these situations, I was presented with a task by my boss and my first reaction was "no way, not comfortable, don't want to do it." Of course this was my internal reaction, my outward response was positive and obedient.

If I had to do it over again, I would have stood up to Ruben and let him pay the penalty for returning the VCR late. In the case of Merlin I still would have taken him, but I would have made sure to check in with him more often during the day, and assumed nothing about what he did or didn't know.

I can tell you this for sure, the next time the boss asks for a favor and a big concert is involved; I am going to think it through before giving any answer at all. I advise you do the same.

Do people ever ask you to do things with which you are not comfortable for whatever reason?

Think about this. You've probably asked someone to do something, and their reaction was either a direct "I'm not comfortable with that," or a look that told you the same. In those cases you accommodated the request, yet for some reason most people think others won't do the same for them.

The next time a discomforting request comes your way, say something. No matter the reaction you get, it won't be worse than getting smacked around by a bunch of townies.

Stephen S. Nazarian

30 – WANDER INTO THE WEEDS

In the summer of 1980 I was eleven years old. I had played some summer little league, and plenty of pickup baseball games around the neighborhood, but no Babe Ruth was I. In fact my lack of talent on the diamond was something that my teammates had regularly pointed out.

One Saturday my Dad asked me if I would like to go with him to play softball with some medical residents. My father was one of the local pediatricians in the suburb of Rochester NY where I grew up, and one of the things he did was teach pediatric residents in his office. Every so often he would be invited to some resident event, and this particular weekend the invitation was to join them for an informal softball game.

We hopped into Dad's brown Ford Pinto and headed off to the park.

MY DAD IS ONE OF THOSE GUYS WHO IS NEVER ON TIME; HE IS ALWAYS EARLY.

I think it stems from growing up in New Jersey where everything takes longer than it should.

The day was sunny and we drove with the windows down since it would be six more years before the Nazarians would own a car with air conditioning (not that anyone was counting).

We arrived at the park a full 15 minutes before the appointed time but not too long after, young doctors started showing up in a steady stream. Some of the residents brought friends with them and a few of these friends were law students. I only remember this because later in the day when we actually got to playing, the law students were blamed for all questionable plays and calls.

Once a critical mass of players had arrived, we set about the task of picking teams. I got picked early because there was some idea that a younger kid would be valuable; they had clearly never seen me play.

As the teams were being finalized, a few more players trickled in, and without too much more trouble, we were ready to play, almost. People grabbed their hats, gloves and bats from their cars and headed onto the field.

THERE WAS ONLY ONE PROBLEM – NOBODY HAD A SOFTBALL. NOBODY.

Furthermore we couldn't call anyone since this was 1980, and there were no cell phones, not even the Gordon Gekko brick phone. All we could do is wait for more people to show up and hope one of them had a ball.

I don't know if you've ever been stuck anywhere with of a group of doctors, but what happens is, in the absence of anything else to do, they will immediately revert to talking about medicine, they really can't help it. And so they did – start enthusiastically talking about medicine. This went on for what seemed like forever (probably 5 minutes) when I began looking around for something more interesting to do.

I AM A HIGHLY OBSERVANT PERSON. I SEE ALL THE DETAILS OF THE THINGS AROUND ME; I CAN'T HELP IT I JUST DO.

So, as I sat on one of the low railroad ties that bordered the parking lot I began to look around. What happened next was one of those "a-ha" moments you remember forever.

As my eyes scanned the horizon to the drone of medical banter, I noticed that the entire outfield, as well as the third-base side of the field, was surrounded by tall weeds. I had played enough bad neighborhood baseball to know that such geography is exactly where balls go, but from which they rarely return. So I wandered off into the weeds determined to find a softball, get the game going, and end the medicinal rap session.

Since it was 1980, nobody noticed nor cared that the only kid in the group (literally) wandered off into the weeds. Off I went and about 5 minutes later I emerged with two pristine softballs, one of which was so clean it only had a single mark where it had been hit, just once.

As I presented the two balls to the gathered medical masses, there was a collective cheer and the game began. I don't remember much else about the game other than the aforementioned disparaging of the lawyers.

I can't imagine my playing was any good at all, but I do remember being well regarded by a group of adults more than twice my age, because I was the kid who not only put together the idea that there might be a ball out there to use, but actually went out and found it.

How often are any of us in a situation where we have an idea to solve the problem, but we stay silent for fear of it not working?

HOW OFTEN DO WE CHOOSE NOT TO WANDER INTO THE WEEDS?

I had the advantage of really having nothing to lose, but that didn't change the odds of being successful. I could have just as easily found nothing in the weeds, but standing in the parking lot would have guaranteed that.

The next time you have a thought or an idea, no matter how absurd, take a deep breath and wander into the weeds. You just might be surprised at what you'll find and how valuable it will be to those around you.

Welcome to the week called "you finally say or do something." We all have ideas that pop into our heads, but much of the time we say nothing (or do nothing) for fear of our audience not understanding.

This week, every time you have an idea, blurt it out. Try not to interrupt, but don't wait too long. If you can't get it out quickly, write it down and send a memo, write an email or just write the idea on a whiteboard or bulletin board. If it is something you can just go do, go do it.

Wayne Gretzky famously said, "You will miss 100% of the shots that you do not take." This is the week you start taking shots.

Many of them you will miss, but the ones that hit home, the ones that last week would have never been considered, will make your day. Kind of like a kid who found a softball in the weeds and saved the game.

Stephen S. Nazarian

31 – DRIVE BY WIRE

There is a term in the car world – *Drive By Wire*. Wikipedia defines Drive By Wire as follows:

Technology in the automotive industry refers to the use of electrical or electro-mechanical systems for performing vehicle functions traditionally achieved by mechanical linkages/actuators. This technology replaces the traditional mechanical control systems with electronic control systems using electromechanical actuators and human-machine interfaces such as pedal and steering feel emulators. Hence, the traditional components such as the steering column, intermediate shafts, pumps, hoses, belts, coolers and vacuum servos and master cylinders are eliminated from the vehicle. This is similar to the fly by wire systems used widely in the aviation industry.

IN THE SUMMER OF 1997 I HAD MY OWN DRIVE BY WIRE EXPERIENCE AND IT IS ONE THAT I WILL NEVER FORGET.

In the spring of 1997 I purchased a 1973 Porsche 911-T Targa. It was silver with a back interior, black Targa convertible roof and black Fuchs wheels.

Although pretty good looking, there was no doubt that this car was going to be a project. In fact, on the drive home from where I purchased it, the car overheated and I had to call my friend Chip to come get me with a towrope. This was going to be a hobby, not my daily driver.

I spent a few months tinkering with the car.

911s from this area are by definition "air cooled" however what that really means is that they are oil cooled (the engine uses 11 quarts of oil). I fixed the problems with the oil cooling, replaced a fuel line and a few other things, working towards getting the car on the road.

I read magazines and ordered catalogs trying to learn as much as I could about early 1970s 911s, and after patching up most of the critical systems it was time for a road trip.

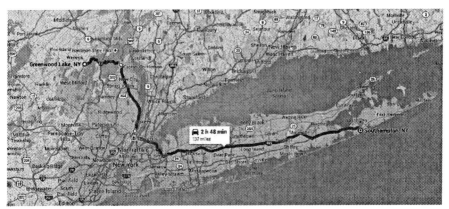

The route from Greenwood Lake to Southampton

One weekend my friend Tim invited me out to his house in the Hamptons for the day, and if there was ever a place to drive your topless Porsche, the Southampton NY, is that place.

When I said that most of the critical systems were fixed, here is what I meant:

- Engine – OK
- Transmission – OK
- Steering – OK
- Brakes – Marginal, such that I regularly had to supplement what I got from the pedal with the hand brake, but since most of the trip was on the highway I wasn't too concerned
- Everything else – Seemed to be OK

I woke on Saturday morning, did a final check around the car and headed out on the 137-mile journey. I zipped through the curves of Harriman State Park, down the Palisades Parkway, over the George Washington Bridge, then the Throg's Neck Bridge onto Long Island.

AROUND 11:00AM I PULLED INTO TIM'S DRIVEWAY IN SOUTHAMPTON.

We hung out for a while and then headed out for lunch. We drove around Southampton for about an hour, me in my '73 Targa, and Tim in his '94 Porsche 911 Speedster. We pulled into a restaurant and had a nice lunch. After we ate, we headed out on the streets again and zoomed around for another forty-five minutes before heading back to Tim's house.

We hung out by the pool for the balance of the afternoon, had a nice dinner on the patio, and at 7:00 I hopped back into the Targa to head home.

As ubiquitous as the 911 is, it still gets attention pretty much everywhere you go. Of course in the Hamptons, Tim's shiny black Speedster was attracting more eyeballs than my comparatively shabby Targa, but on the drive out, I had received dozens of waves, thumbs-up and a few toots of the horn.

HEADING HOME, I DROVE THE LENGTH OF LONG ISLAND INTO THE WESTERN SUN, TOP DOWN, TUNES ON, AND WARM WIND IN MY HAIR. LIFE WAS GOOD.

As I crossed the upper level George Washington Bridge into New Jersey, I passed a convertible Chrysler LeBaron filled with four young ladies. They clearly liked my car, and I'd like to think they thought I was okay too.

I zoomed ahead, buoyed by the positive shot to my ego, leaning into the curved ramp that leads from the upper GWB onto the Palisades Parkway north. I passed the "last gas in NJ" station that always has a long line, and continued cruising comfortably in the left lane.

Around a bend in the highway, I came up quickly on the backside of a slow moving pickup truck, forcing me to downshift and use both of my brake choices to avoid rear-ending the slothsom fellow. When he finally moved out of my way, I was really ready to gun it, so I dropped a gear, let out the clutch and punched the gas to the floor.

BUT NOTHING HAPPENED.

The accelerator was dead. The pedal moved in and out like it was supposed to, but the engine was not responding at all. I pushed the clutch in and coasted, but as the speedometer showed me slowing down, the tachometer was showing my engine stuck at idle.

I pulled into the right lane as quickly as I could do so safely, and then onto the shoulder. Cars were whipping by so fast and so close that I couldn't even get out of the car.

I knew that there was another gas station a few miles up the road, so using only the idle speed of the engine, I put on my hazards, shifted into first and slowly let out the clutch. The car was going about 12 miles an hour when I successfully shifted into second without stalling.

AND THERE I STAYED, GOING 18 MPH, IN THE RIGHT LANE, MY HAZARD LIGHTS POUNDING OUT THE HEARTBEAT OF MECHANICAL FAILURE.

I was nearly rear-ended several times, as I covered the 5 miles to the gas station, and I received several not-so-friendly horn honks, and more than one "pointed gesture."

As I approached the gas station, I realized that I had another problem. The station was in the median between the north and south-bound lanes of the parkway, so I was going to have to cross the fast lane to get over there.

Honking horns and middle fingers notwithstanding, I managed to pull my sad little German two-seater into the gas station without incident. I parked the car, killed the engine and got out to sort through my options.

If you're not aware, the design of the 911 evolved from the humble Volkswagen Beetle, so the engine is in the back of the car. I walked around to the trunk (which is actually the hood), popped the latch and had a look. Everything looked to be in order, so I went back and started her up. With the engine running, I started poking around to see if I could find the throttle, which I did almost immediately. Pushing on a spring-loaded lever that was connected to the engine, via a network of stainless steel rods, I could easily rev the engine just like the gas pedal was supposed to.

The 911 throttle and connecting rods

It was at this time I remembered reading about a $12 part in one of my catalogs that claimed to, "permanently fix the firewall throttle linkage failure problem, so common to early 1970s 911s." There was no way I was going to fix that problem at a parkway gas station. Furthermore, 911s can't be towed; they must be put on a flatbed – something I was in no position to pay for.

It was going on 9:00pm, the sun was going down and there was literally nobody for me to call. My previous 911 rescue friend Chip had since moved to Texas.

With the engine purring at idle and the hood propped open, I went around the front of the car to see what I might have in trunk to help me "MacGyver" my way out of this situation.

I opened the trunk and found a cardboard box containing a brown, six-foot extension cord and a couple of cotton rags, that's it.

As I stood beside my hobbled little toy, trying to come up with a way to cover the

This was all I found

thirty or so miles back to my bed, karma decided to kick me in the shorts. The previously observed "convertible LeBaron full of ladies" rolled by me in full giggle, proceeding to the gas pumps for a fill-up; it was a new "personal best" in humiliation.

I TURNED MY WOUNDED EGO BACK TOWARDS MY EQUALLY WOUNDED CAR AND GOT BUSY SOLVING THE PROBLEM AT HAND.

I took the extension cord, and using the tiny Swiss Army Knife on my keychain, I cut off both the plug and receptacle ends. I then pulled the two wires apart, and tied them together at one end. The result was a nearly twelve-foot-long "rope." I tied the wire to the lever that revved the engine, and threaded it through a vent hole in the hood. I closed the hood and tossed the wire into the driver's seat, through the open Targa top.

All I had to do was tie the wire to the gas pedal and I would have effectively bypassed the broken throttle cable. I opened the driver side door to finish the job, but the wire only reached the front edge of the driver's seat. It was two and a half feet too short, ugh. I was wearing loafers, so there were no shoelaces to be put into service.

I got in anyway, started the engine and tugged on the wire. Sure enough the engine revved, so that was good. I needed my right hand for the shifter and the emergency brake. I needed my left hand for the steering wheel. I needed my left foot for the clutch and I needed my right foot for the regular brake.

IN THE END I HAD NO CHOICE BUT TO TIE A KNOT AT THE END OF THE WIRE AND PUT IT BETWEEN MY TEETH.

Sitting in the driver's seat of my German-engineered sports car, I put the shifter in first, and as I let out the clutch I turned my entire head to the left to rev the engine.

It worked, but I must have looked funny as hell as I drove along, wire in mouth, and my head positioned in such a way that any passing doctor would have instantly diagnosed me with some kind of rare palsy. I made it to the exit where I got off the highway to drive through Harriman State Park, but then something else happened. With no warning or other indication, the car lost a lot of its power, but it was still moving, so I kept going.

HALF AN HOUR LATER I WAS SAFELY IN MY DRIVEWAY.

The next morning I popped the hood and it was easy to see what had happened. The wire had slipped and popped off one of the stainless steel rods, effectively cutting fuel from three of the cylinders. I had driven the last fifteen miles on half an engine.

Looking back, the decision to purchase of a quarter-century old project sports car at the same time my house project didn't yet have a functioning kitchen was probably a bad one.

Cars are a pain in the ass, and if you choose to own something other than a modern, reliable model; be ready to pay up, get clever or both. In 1999 I sold the Porsche to support my move back to Rochester.

In 2014 I bought a thirty-year-old German convertible on eBay, and for every hour I have driven it, I have spent at least four hours working on it. I guess some people never learn; and I wouldn't have it any other way.

There are things in our lives that we must do and conversely there are things that we want to do. If you graphed all of these things on a curve, you'd quickly find that you spend most of your life on the "must do" side.

This is the week you pick one of those "want to" things and start making it happen. It does not need to be expensive, or complicated. It must simply be something you want to do, acquire or experience that seems too frivolous to pursue. News flash – if it is important to you, it's not frivolous.

Fair warning - if you do this, you might find yourself stranded by the side of the road with nothing more that an extension cord to save you. And wouldn't that be awesome?

32 – CONNECTION JUNCTION (THE GREATEST FUNCTION)

In the 1970s when the Alstom Corporation was developing the French high-speed train, the TGV (Train à Grande Vitesse), they encountered unexpected, high-speed, problems with the way train cars connect to each other. They solved these problems in an unconventional way.

Since the beginning of trains, all train cars shared the same basic layout for their wheels. Each car has two "trucks" that are connected to the underside of the train, and under the trucks are the two pairs of wheels. Before the TGV, all trains were laid out this way.

The improved TGV design uses a single truck, mounted between two adjacent cars and allows for those cars to better articulate as the curve of the track dictates. The new approach, although very simple, turned conventional thinking on its ear while solving all the problems.

The solution came from a fresh re-thinking of the connection between two train cars. The cars themselves were not the problem, but rather the outdated connection between them was.

Back in the 1990s, I was on a company ski trip in Vermont. At one point in the day, I found myself sharing a chairlift with one of our mechanical engineers. As we rode I verbalized a thought I was having about the cable that held up the chairlift, and how I wasn't convinced that it could hold all the weight. The engineer (his name was Dave) rather quickly informed me that I was correct, and that the steel in the cable wasn't nearly strong enough to perform the task. Now that he had provoked me I had to ask:

Steel cable or "Wire Rope" used in ski lifts

"IF THE CABLE ISN'T STRONG ENOUGH, THE HOW THE HECK ARE WE RIDING UP THE MOUNTAIN ON IT RIGHT NOW?"

He went on to explain that the strength of the cable was only partly due to the steel, but the majority of the strength came from the friction between the multiple sets of twisted wires.

Just think about that for a minute. The majority of the strength comes from the connection (in this case friction) between the wires, not the wires themselves. What's even more interesting is that without the wires present, the friction does not exist at all.

In 1999, when I decided to propose to my wife, I spent some time shopping for a diamond ring. I went from store to store looking at hundreds of options, but none of them seemed right.

One day I stopped into a small independent jewelry store at the suggestion of a friend. The owner of the store started to go through his standard diamond ring pitch, but before he got too far, I was distracted (shocking I know) by some pieces in the next case over.

Every display case in the store was neat and orderly, except for this one. This particular display looked like the jewelry equivalent of a garage sale.

He noticed my wandering gaze and said, "oh, are you interested in estate pieces?" The case that caught my eye was a hodge-podge of different pieces that had come from estates. "Estate piece" is jewelry speak for "used." There were pins, broaches, necklaces, earrings, and all the way down on the left, there were some rings. As my eyes passed over all the things I was not interested in, they landed on (what I now know is) an approximately 100-year-old engagement ring that literally spoke to me.

I ASKED TO SEE IT AND MY SEARCH WAS OVER.

From that moment on I have never found any jewelry for my wife Emily – jewelry for her has always found me. Once I let a different approach to the relationship (connection) between the ring and me happen, I found exactly what I was looking for. I thought I was shopping for a ring, but in fact I was wandering, so that specific ring could find me.

I do most of the cooking in our family and as a result I do most of the grocery shopping. Whenever we are having friends over for dinner, I head off to the store or public market – not so much with a list, but rather an idea.

I know the personalities, likes and dislikes of those I am going to serve. I know that different things are available at different times of the year. And I also know that one anchor ingredient can be the inspiration for an entire meal.

Having friends over for dinner is far more about the friends than it is the dinner, so I let the anticipated fellowship (connection) of the evening inform my buying, and in turn the meal becomes just one more factor in the equation of the encounter. In this case the dinner isn't finding me as much as I am on a guided, fairly organic and random journey.

THE JOURNEY IS OVER WHEN THE MENU HAS BUILT ITSELF.

These little passages may seem to be all over the map. From train and ski lift engineering, to engagement ring and dinner party shopping. You may finally have all the evidence you need to prove that I am a nut, but hear me out.

Think about all the important and meaningful things in your life. Really think about them. Very little of value comes from the individual person or thing, the value, the love, the meaning all come from the connections.

These connections, much like the friction in the ski lift cable, simply do not exist without those making them, but what they make is what endures. It is a bit of a paradox I admit, but it is nonetheless true.

So, pay attention to the connections in your life. Treasure them, cherish them and pay them the respect and reverence they deserve. Our time here is short, and we never know when all the other strands of wire, in that steel cable we call life, will be gone, taking the strength-giving friction with them.

Now, for those who are old enough to remember, I encourage you to go to YouTube and look up the Schoolhouse Rock song, *Conjunction Junction*, which inspired the title of this chapter. Of course if you look closely, you'll see that all the trains have the old-style trucks. It is my hope you'll never look at trains, or relationships the same – ever again.

Nobody likes taking inventory, but this week that is your task. Grab a notebook, an index card or even just a scrap of paper and take the time to write down all of your important connections as you interact with them. Keep the paper with you all week.

Some connections will be obvious, but others will be much harder to identify. It is the subtle ones that will surprise you, both because you may have never noticed them, but also because they might be really important once you see them clearly.

At the end of the week, that which appeared so normal before should take on an entirely new dimension. Before you venture into the next chapter, your sense for the depth, complexity and importance of connections should be as new and fresh as a ride up a chair lift on a crisp winter's day.

33 – KNOW YOUR LIMITS

Back in the early 1990s I worked in a company that had about 400 employees, 300 in the factory and 100 in the office. In the office area we had a nice break room where small groups of coworkers could sit at one of the half-dozen tables while eating lunch.

A few times a week, several of us from the marketing department would eat together, and over time a few traditions developed. My favorite came on Tuesdays when the local newspaper would publish all the wedding photos from the previous weekend. We would pass the paper around the table and then vote for the winner of the: "Thank goodness she's off the street" award.

CHILDISH? YES IT WAS, BUT WE WERE ALL IN OUR EARLY TWENTIES, AND TO BE HONEST THERE WAS ALMOST ALWAYS A CLEAR WINNER – WOOF.

Given the place in time, there was a fashion trend that was as risky as it was popular. I am not talking about spiked clothing or creative piercings – I am referring to the practice of wearing a long sweater over a pair of tight stirrup pants or leggings.

One day in the break room, my cheeky marketing brethren and I were enjoying our marginal lunches, when a young woman from purchasing came walking into the room.

We all have clothing that looks good on us, and we all have certain styles and looks that we should avoid. What I'm talking about has nothing to do with style, life choices or genetics. Everyone has a different shape, and those shapes work well with some subset of available fashion. For example, I personally should never wear anything in the neighborhood of a "muscle tee."

So, the lady from purchasing walked in, and went over to the fridge to retrieve her lunch. I guess her bag was on a lower shelf because she bent over rather dramatically, and in doing so showed us all why the sweater-over-the-stirrup-pants look just wasn't right for everyone.

We were all sitting in such a way, that not one of us missed this prescient episode of *What Not To Wear*, and as she rose and walked out of the room we were all at a loss for words.

My friend Chris, who was known for being a straight-shooting, no nonsense gal, inhaled and then calmly said:

"KNOW YOUR LIMITS... WORK WITHIN THEM."

It wasn't perhaps the friendliest thing ever said, but she managed to politely articulate what we were all thinking, and creatively so.

As you well know by this point in the book, I love to work on cars. Even during the "dark times," that four-year period where we owned nothing but minivans, I still liked to pop the hood and fix things myself.

Our gold 1998 Grand Caravan (the least favorite of all the cars I've ever owned) was making a groaning noise. A little basic detective work revealed it was the steering pump.

My least favorite minivan

I discussed it with my wife and we decided that we should just leave it with the mechanic while we went away on vacation the following week (in the other minivan, gulp). After all, I'd never changed a steering pump.

In the days following that discussion, it was bugging me that I was going to have to pay several hundred dollars to simply swap out a pump that involved only two bolts, three hoses and a pulley.

So, the night before we were supposed to leave for vacation, with my wife busy at work, I went to the auto parts store. I got the pump and a new serpentine belt and went to check out. The clerk looked at my purchases and said, "you know you need to pull the pulley off the old pump and put it on the new pump; do you have a pulley-puller?" I had never heard of a "pulley-puller," so I bought one of those too.

I WENT HOME, PUT THE KIDS TO BED, DIALED IN THE CLASSIC ROCK STATION ON THE GARAGE RADIO AND GOT TO WORK.

At the time I did not have a good trolley jack or jack stands; I simply put the front of the van up on ramps. I took off the old belt, unbolted the pump from the engine block and disconnected the hoses; it was then the trouble began.

No matter how I tried, I could not get the old pump out. I couldn't get it out from above, below or the side. I have a better than average sense of spatial relations, but despite nearly an hour of trying it simply would not come out.

Here was the problem. I had removed the belt that drives all the accessories on the car, including the water pump that cools the engine. I couldn't put it back on because the steering pump was off. Oh, did I neglect to mention that in one of my many attempts to extricate the pump that I broke the pulley?

IT WAS 11:30PM, AND I WAS OUT OF OPTIONS. I WAS IN OVER MY HEAD AND I HAD TO ADMIT DEFEAT.

The next morning, as soon as the babysitter arrived, I put on my running shoes and jogged to the mechanic. I explained the situation and they agreed to help, after they stopped laughing. What's worse, because I had functionally disabled the van, I had to pay to have it towed in addition to paying to have it fixed.

It turns out that the only way to get that steering pump out is to put the van up on a rack, drop the suspension and remove several pieces of the exhaust system. Had I known this, I would have never even attempted the job in the first place.

This experience created what we now call Nazarian's first rule of auto repair, which states:

IF THE JOB REQUIRES A TOOL THAT YOU HAVE NEVER USED (OR EVEN HEARD OF), OR ONE THAT YOU DO NOT OWN, YOU SHOULD PROBABLY NOT DO IT YOURSELF.

I know I go on-and-on about boldly taking chances, and moving outside of your comfort zone, but we all have limits and sometimes those limits can be dangerous to exceed. Nazarian's First Rule of Woodworking states:

NO CORDED POWER TOOLS AFTER 10:00PM.

That came out of almost losing my spleen late one night when I was too tired to be drilling bird's eye maple with a 2" Forstner bit. If you're a woodworker, you know what I mean.

So get your hands dirty, utilize all the resources you have available to you and stretch yourself to do better things every day. However, recognize that you are human, you do have limits, and pushing them can sometimes make your situation worse, not better.

Oh, and don't even consider doing any of these things while wearing stirrup pants and a long sweater.

Think back over the last six months. Unless you are a superhero, you can probably come up with a few situations where you either didn't know, or exceeded your own limits. We all do it and the reasons vary from ignorance to hubris or simple unchecked enthusiasm.

Once you've made your list, look at it critically and see if you can come up with a few "rules" of your own that, if followed, would have prevented most, or all of the noted events.

Write them down on post-it notes and place them where you can't miss them. You could even have them put on a t-shirt, just make sure it's one that works for you.

34 – CHECK YOUR RECEIPTS

Early one Sunday morning I went to Wegmans (the most amazing grocery store in the world if you're unfamiliar) to get supplies for Mother's day, and to do my regular weekly grocery shopping. You can do this at Wegmans because apart from Thanksgiving and Christmas, they are open 24/7. I had a specific list of what I needed for the day, which I ticked off as I did my usual all-aisle, zigzag through the store.

I was purchasing several items that I don't buy regularly, so I had no real feel for the total as the checkout kid scanned and bagged the last items. I can also say that despite the coffee I was sipping, I was still in an early Sunday morning fog, since it was only 6:40am.

He announced the total, I reflexively swiped my card and then what he said finally clicked – $270! Man, that seemed steep, but the transaction was complete, he was handing me my receipt and had already begun scanning the next order. I stumbled forward to scrutinize the yard-long list of my purchases.

Line by line everything looked normal until I got to the case of Wegmans brand coffee pods for $29.99. I had purchased one, but somehow the checkout kid had rung me up for five.

A QUICK STOP AT CUSTOMER SERVICE AND MY $270 BILL WAS DOWN TO $150 – THAT'S MORE LIKE IT!

Of course it got me thinking about how many times the total is "about what I expected" and how often it might be wrong, either in their favor or mine. I do pay close attention as they enter produce codes since the price of broccoli crowns is about one-tenth that of pine nuts, despite the similarity of their codes.

Several years ago my in-laws were visiting from Virginia, where they could not get decent Chinese food. So every time they came to visit, a night of takeout from the *Joy Luck Garden* was always in the plan. This time there were going to be five of us for dinner, my in-laws, me, Emily and Emily's aunt Suzanne.

My wife called in the order, and I heard her having some trouble on the phone articulating what we wanted, but that was nothing new. When it came time to go get the food, my father-in-law pressed his credit card into my hand and insisted that he pay. I learned very early on not to argue with my father-in-law.

When I arrived at the restaurant, it wasn't too busy. There were a few tables of people towards the back and sitting at a round table right next to the pickup counter were four NY State Troopers.

I gave my name to the man at the counter; he grabbed the tag off the big bag of food and rang it up. Just like that morning in the grocery store, I wasn't paying too close attention to what he said.

I hate using other people's credit cards; even with permission it feels like I'm stealing something. I handed over my father-in-law's card, they swiped it, but as they handed me the receipt to sign I noticed a problem.

THE TOTAL WAS $87! I LOOKED UP AND ASKED "CAN YOU READ THE ORDER BACK TO ME PLEASE?" THIS IS THE CONVERSATION THAT FOLLOWED:

JLG: One order shrimp lo-mein, one order General Tso chicken, one order moo-shoo pork, one order house special fried rice, one order broccoli garlic sauce, five orders steamed dumpling.

Me: Five orders steamed dumplings?

JLG: Yes, lady on phone was very specific!

Me: That doesn't even make any sense, five orders of dumplings with five entrees. That's thirty dumplings. That's a lot of dumplings.

JLG: (with a very condescending look and tone) Maybe more people coming than you think?

The subtext of the last statement was basically "they sent you to pick-up the food, perhaps you're not as in-the-know as you think you are, messenger boy."

As I weighed my options I realized what had happened, my wife had tried to place a single order for five dumplings (one for each of us), but since there were six to an order, the language barrier produced the situation I've just described.

I looked at Mr. Joy Luck Garden, I looked at the "stolen" credit card on the counter, and glanced over at the four NY State Troopers. I figured the best way out was to just shut-up and take the dumplings, which I did.

MY FATHER-IN-LAW THOUGHT THE WHOLE STORY WAS HILARIOUS, AND TOLD IT EVERY TIME HE ENCOUNTERED CHINESE FOOD FOR THE REST OF HIS LIFE. WHEW!

Some time in 2014, I was again in the Penfield Wegmans with my daughter Charlotte. As I was working my way through the checkout process, she had gone to the sub counter to pick up a large sub that we would all share for lunch.

She returned to my checkout line with the sub just as I was finishing up. I swiped, signed and we were on our way. As we walked towards the door, Charlotte looked up and me and said "Dad, we didn't pay for the sub!"

A funny thing happens in situations like this. Every part of our human nature fires off at once. Of course the right thing to do is to go back and pay for the sub. But there is that part of you that says "ugh, I just spent $185 on this cart full of food and I really don't want to get back in that line, and I'm sure I've overpaid by more than the cost of the $7.00 sub over the years in wrong produce codes alone."

Then there is that little rebel-without-a-cause part of us that wants to "get away" with something just for the thrill of it. Of course all of these thoughts fly through your mind in about ¾ of a second.

I TURNED TO MY TWELVE-YEAR-OLD DAUGHTER AND SAID, "FOLLOW ME."

We walked over the Customer Service and paid for the sub. Given the spectrum of options that flood our flawed human minds, I absolutely needed to show my daughter what the right choice was. In the end that is probably what I would have done either way, but it is important to acknowledge the internal conflicts and temptations we all face every day. If you claim that you don't have thoughts like this, you are either lying or an alien.

I know we all would publicly say "of course I would go back and pay for the sub," but if we are truly honest with ourselves, we know we have other thoughts, other options. Charlotte and I realized the problem while we were still in the store, but what if we had been in the car, or already home? I haven't personally spent too much time in retail, but I did enough as a teenager to tell you that people choose the "other path" all the time. We are all presented with choices every day. Every one has a short-term and a long-term result, which are usually at odds with each other. So with all of this said I have two pieces of life-learned advice:

CHECK YOUR RECEIPTS, EVERY TIME YOU BUY ANYTHING.

-AND-

MAKE YOUR DECISIONS AS IF AN IMPRESSIONABLE TWELVE-YEAR-OLD IS WATCHING EVERY ONE.

If you add these two practices to your daily life, you will make sure that life doesn't cheat you, but more importantly you will sleep well at night knowing that you didn't cheat yourself out of the life you want to live. Because in the end – there are probably more people coming than you think!

For the next seven days, get a receipt from every transaction and keep them all. Treat the coming week like a business trip for which you must turn in every bit of transactional documentation.

Get an envelope and keep it in your pocket, purse or bag and place each receipt inside as you collect them.

At the end of the week, lay them all out on your kitchen table, in order, and look at them – with a critical eye.

Are you happy with all your choices? In every case did you actually pay for what you got? Is there anything you want to return or exchange?

Many of our experiences and exchanges are fleeting. We can learn a lot by simply reviewing the documentation that typically ends up as garbage or dryer lint.

I'm not saying you have to, but if you did this for a few weeks in a row I'm betting you will start to see a real change in how you spend your money, and that can't be bad.

35 – HOARD IN MODERATION

Every once in a while flipping through the channels, I stop on that show about hoarders. I know the people on that show have a serious psychological condition, and that it defies all normal logic, but it certainly does make you think about what you choose to keep and what you choose to discard.

One summer as a teenager I spent two weeks at Boy Scout camp in the Adirondacks. The first week was traditional camp where we slept in platform tents, worked on merit badges, frolicked in the lake and played with all forms of fire. The second week was a fifty-mile canoe trip with a few intrepid fathers, and about half of the kids from week one.

Every Thursday the traditional camp staff had the day off, so all the campers, and their leaders, had to head out on "Trail day." From Thursday morning until noon Friday, we all had to pack up, and hit the trail while the staff went into town to spend their meager paychecks.

Massawepie Scout Camp is nearly 5,000 acres, so there are plenty of places to hike to for a night. On Wednesday evening we were given our provisions, and first thing Thursday morning we headed out.

We hiked for the morning, ate lunch, made camp, swam in a pond, cooked dinner, went to bed, made breakfast, broke camp and hiked back. One of the things we had been given for dinner was instant French onion soup. It was hot that day so we decided not to make the soup, but instead of throwing it away, I tucked the four packets into my backpack.

TRAIL DAY CAME AND WENT, THE REGULAR CAMP WEEK CAME TO AN END AND WE HEADED OUT ON THE CANOE TRIP.

Day one of the trip was fine, but as we paddled along on day two, we started to have some trouble. We had to cover ten miles that day, and soon after we shoved off, the sun disappeared, the temperature dropped, and it began to rain. It rained all morning and by the time we stopped for lunch, many of the scouts had blue lips and were shivering.

If you've never done any serious camping, you probably don't know that the most dangerous conditions for hypothermia are actually 40-60 degrees and rain, not freezing cold.

IT HAD BEEN 50 AND RAINING FOR FOUR HOURS.

We tied up the canoes on an island in the middle of the lake that we were traversing, and set up two dining flys so we could all get out of the rain. Since we were only staying long enough to eat, we chose to not make a fire. Lunch on trips like this was typically some crackers and chicken salad from a can.

A "topo" map of the Saranac Lake Chain where things got wet and cold

The adults and boy leaders discussed the situation, trying to decide our best and safest plan for the remainder of the day. One of the adults said "I wish we had something hot to serve for lunch."

IT WAS AT THIS POINT I REMEMBERED THE PACKETS OF FRENCH ONION SOUP.

We immediately grabbed two propane stoves and pots from the canoes. We filled the pots with lake water and set them to heat. Once the water had boiled for a few minutes, we turned off the heat and dumped in the packets of soup.

On a good day, Boy Scout issued, powdered French onion soup is pretty bad, but that day it was the best thing ever. Since the group was smaller than the one for which the soup was planned, there was enough for two servings each. We sat under the temporary shelters, ate our crackers, drank our soup and licked every atom of chicken salad out of the cans, despite the risk of cutting our tongues on the sharp edges.

After about an hour, the rain started to lighten-up, and to the west we could see slivers of blue sky and sunshine. We headed back to our canoes and finished the day strong, arriving at our evening campsite right on schedule.

I could have just as easily tossed the four silver bags of powder into the trash five days earlier, but something told me "hang onto those, you might need them someday."

BOY, WAS THAT LITTLE VOICE EVER RIGHT.

When I moved to New York City right after college, one of the things I packed was a long skinny metal box that had once contained a fancy bottle of 12-year-old Johnnie Walker Black whiskey. In this box I had thrown all sorts of random things that defied more specific classification. That was in December 1991.

To this day, I still have the box and it still contains random stuff. Every time I put something together (Ikea furniture, kid bicycle seat, TV wall mount, etc.) and there are extra, optional or left over parts, they go right into the box. Whenever I'm building or fixing something for which I need a part, but I don't know exactly what I need, the first place I look is the box.

My Johnnie Walker box

Several months ago a friend asked me to build him a special stand for an experiment he was doing. The angle of the stand needed to be adjustable. So, before I even started planning I went to the box for inspiration. Sure enough there was a metal bracket in there, from who-knows-what, and it was perfect for what I was trying to do.

Certainly you can save too much stuff and since I like to build and fix stuff, my default is to hold onto most things because "I just might need it someday." Every few years I do a thorough cleaning of my workshop and stuff that has sat quietly gathering dust through two or three cleanings, usually gets recycled or tossed. I even dump out the black box every so often, but that is usually when I'm trying to put in something new that won't fit. That's the rule; if I can't close the lid something else needs to come out first.

You know that drawer in your kitchen that is loaded with paperclips, magnets, takeout menus and other random crap? We all hate that drawer, yet we go to it all the time and it regularly produces what we need.

Too much stuff is too much, yet not enough is not enough. The challenge is finding where that line is for you and your family. It's time to figure out what "hoard in moderation" means to you.

This week, go out and get your very own "Johnnie Walker box" and start loading it up with random stuff that the future you just might need. You can start with the kitchen drawer-o-crap, which is probably due for a cleaning anyway.

If you can't find an empty metal liquor box lying around, you might have to purchase it full and drain it of its contents first. This will also work for tins filled with cookies or candy.

Whatever you must consume to get your container, I can promise you that it will taste better, and provide at least as much satisfaction as powdered French Onion Soup on a cold rainy day.

---

36 – THE WHOLE TRUTH, & NOTHING BUT THE TRUTH

In 1995 I read the novel *Snow Falling on Cedars* by David Guterson. In addition to it being a great read, it helped me settle a conflict that my twenty-something brain had been struggling with. The book tells the story of a murder and the trial that follows, but (being a thriller) everything is not what it appears to be.

In the end, the whole truth is revealed and justice is served, but not before dozens of half-truths and misunderstandings damage a lot of relationships. I would tell you more, but it is a great book; you should read it. If you're feeling lazy, they made a movie in 1999 staring Ethan Hawke.

The idea that the book settled for me was the same one that a similar experience settled for my father-in-law ten years later. His story is a much better one then mine, so that's the one I'm going to tell.

The oath that witnesses swear when taking the stand in an American legal proceeding is:

DO YOU SWEAR TO TELL THE TRUTH, THE WHOLE TRUTH, AND NOTHING BUT THE TRUTH, SO HELP YOU GOD?

We all generally understand what this means, but I think the "whole truth" portion is the part that is least understood and quite possibly the most important. A partial truth may in fact be more damaging than a lie, since at least a lie can be legitimately contradicted.

My father-in-law was born in 1925. He lived through World War II, served in the Navy during the Korean Conflict, was a surgeon on Long Island for more than three decades, and with his lovely wife raised twelve children. That is not a typo, twelve children.

He was brought up in a fairly strict Roman Catholic household, and throughout his life was a firm believer in conservative political philosophy. He was resolute that those legitimately convicted of the greatest crimes, deserved to pay the ultimate price.

My Father-in-law with my kids burying a body (actually they're planting onions)

SIMPLY PUT... HE BELIEVED STRONGLY IN THE DEATH PENALTY.

The 1992 movie *My Cousin Vinny* told the story of two college students from New York City, on a road trip through rural Alabama. As the film opens the two main characters walk into a convenience store called the *Sac-O-Suds* to pick up some provisions. As they drive away two things occur:

1. One of the lead characters puts his hand in his jacket pocket and realizes that he accidentally shoplifted two cans of tuna

2. Two other characters enter the *Sac-O-Suds* to rob it and end up killing a clerk in the process

The balance of the movie is made up of a confession, a retraction, a defense lawyer cousin named Vinny Gambini, madcap interactions with the southern townsfolk, a carnival of a trial and ultimately an acquittal.

IF YOU HAVEN'T SEEN THE MOVIE IT REALLY IS QUITE ENTERTAINING. I RECOMMEND IT HIGHLY.

Even though everyone watching the movie knows that the two main characters are innocent, the evidence against them is both voluminous and compelling. They are being tried for capital murder and until the final scenes of the film; it looks like the two are headed for death row.

Only after Cousin Vinny's fiancé (Mona Lisa Vito) is able to shed some additional light on the evidence presented, does the "whole truth" become clear.

For the majority of the movie we all know that they are innocent, but the justice system is seeing just the opposite. The film is so fun that you pretty much know things are going to get better, and in the end it is just a story, but it does make you think about how things happen in real crimes and trials.

My father-in-law loved a good movie. He had seen enough of the evolution of cinema that even in 2010 he still called them "flickers." After he saw *My Cousin Vinny* though, he got to thinking about our justice system. Not too long after that he made a decision:

HE WOULD NO LONGER BE A SUPPORTER OF THE DEATH PENALTY, FOR ANY CRIME, NO MATTER WHAT.

What he concluded was that you could never know for sure what actually happened in a situation that you yourself didn't personally witness. As I said earlier, a partial truth is a dangerous thing since the incomplete story is still true, but absent of details that could change your conclusions.

My wife and I have learned this in parenting our four children, that it is usually enlightening to discover the complete picture before placing any blame or issuing any punishments.

We all receive volumes of information from different sources every day. Research has shown that we tend to hear what we want in things, and making matters worse, we lean towards believing the first version of any story we hear.

THE IDEA OF A NEUTRAL OR UNBIASED PERSON IS A FANTASY. WE ARE INHERENTLY BIASED BY THE LIVES WE'VE LIVED.

Both *Snow Falling On Cedars* and *My Cousin Vinny* are perfect examples of this phenomenon taken to the extreme, but what about the smaller stuff?

Before you make an accusation, draw a conclusion or otherwise make up your mind about someone or something:

TAKE THE TIME TO COLLECT THE WHOLE TRUTH.

You wouldn't listen to a song played with only some of the notes and you wouldn't eat a dish made with only some of the ingredients. Make your decisions based on as much information as you can get. When you do, you will avoid condemning the wrong child to a week of being grounded, or worse.

And here's an idea: perhaps *My Cousin Vinny* should be played in the waiting room for all those called to jury duty. Certainly everyone would have a good time, but maybe just maybe, the best justice system in the world would get just a little bit better.

There is a concept called the "5 whys," which basically states that, you can't get to the bottom of any answer to a question until you ask "why" five times.

In the simplest situations it is overkill. If you come in from the outside soaking wet and someone asks "why are you wet?" and respond "because it is raining" there isn't really anything more to learn; however, in many situations there is.

This week I want you to ask why, at least once but as may as five times before you act, react or respond to any answer or piece of information you receive.

Yes, it will be annoying, but you'll be surprised how quickly a few follow-up questions will improve the accuracy of your actions.

If you end up in trouble, just call Cousin Vinny – he'll know what to do.

37 – NEVER SAY NO TO A TEENAGER

My Dad never said no to his teenage children. That may sound like a recipe for parenting disaster, a formula for the worst of the spoiled-brat entitled generation, but there is much more to it.

Teenagers are funny creatures. They live in an awkward no-man's-land that partly wants to be all grown up, and at the same time still a kid. They want all the power of adulthood, and none of the responsibilities. They scurry to the outer edges of all the known boundaries, seeking to push every one to the breaking point. This all seems completely logical and normal to the teenager, while at the same time driving parents to consider tequila as a regular beverage choice.

Teenagers want to do things and go places. They want freedom, autonomy and anonymity.

> *TEENAGERS WANT THEIR PARENTS TO EXIST JUST LONG ENOUGH TO GIVE THEM $25 AND DRIVE THEM TO WHEREVER IT IS THEY WANT TO GO; AND THEN PROMPTLY DISAPPEAR.*

I know all these things because I was once a teenager, but I grew up in a house where my father never said no to us. If we asked for something, or to do something, my Dad would simply send us away with the following charge:

> *GO UP TO YOUR ROOM WITH A PENCIL AND PAPER AND MAKE A PLAN. WHEN YOU'RE DONE WITH YOUR PLAN, BRING IT BACK TO ME AND WE'LL DISCUSS IT.*

Every household has both spoken and unspoken rules. Everyone in a family knows what is going to fly and what isn't. So, when my Dad sent us off to "make a plan" he knew exactly what he was doing.

He was giving us the autonomy we all so fervently sought, but he was doing it within the context of the known "rules of the house." As I would sit at my desk working on a plan, I would typically encounter a step that I knew was never going to garner support, or as they say in Washington D.C. "never make it out of committee."

MY DAD'S RESPONSE TO THE QUESTIONABLE TEENAGE REQUEST WAS BOTH SUBTLE AND BRILLIANT.

He never had to say no, because most of the time, the inevitable "no" was discovered in the process of making the plan. My brother, sister or I would be sitting at our desks and arrive at the conclusion that "Dad is never going to say yes to this part of the plan," and there it would die, at our hands not his.

Of course if we made it through the plan without a deal-breaker, then the discussion would take place and usually end with a (albeit qualified) yes.

When our daughter Charlotte was born in June of 2000, my Dad offered only one piece of unsolicited advice. He said: "make no mistake, you start raising your teenagers today." Although that may seem a bit extreme he was right, because the expectations, the aforementioned "house rules" are established over years and years of reinforcement, not just a single stern conversation with a ten-year-old.

The composer Igor Stravinski once famously said: "A good composer does not imitate... he steals." Ironically, in the years since, several other composers have been credited with paraphrases of his statement; I guess they took him seriously. With respect to my father's approach to parenting teenagers, I plan on doing nothing short of straight-out stealing.

By empowering teenagers to come to their own conclusions about things that they want, while at the same time acknowledging the functional and emotional things that they need, my Dad never had to say no. He didn't manage, endure nor survive the teenage years of his children, he spent the entire time helping us grow up. We never saw it coming, but now that all three of us have teenagers of our own, we're awfully glad to have a plan. One that we know is going to work.

The teenaged Nazarians lost in the 1980s

If you have children or even if you don't, the idea of never saying no is useful in many contexts.

When managing people I have found that the most effective way to answer a question is to not answer it at all. Instead, empower the asker to answer it on their own.

For the next week, every time someone comes to you seeking an answer to a question or permission to do something, refuse to answer. Instead, send them away to make a plan.

If you do this enough, you'll soon find that they are coming to you less and less. Not because they don't have requests, but because they are figuring things out on their own. When they do come to you, you'll find that instead of asking for an answer, they will be asking to discuss their plan.

In my experience, once they get to that point, it is no longer a matter of not saying no, but rather figuring out how to say yes.

Stephen S. Nazarian

38 – BORDER SECURITY

My kids love to cook. From the time they could get their elbows above the counter, all four of them have enjoyed experimenting in the kitchen, and they are getting pretty good.

One day a few years ago, one of them asked if they could make grilled cheese. I said that they could get started, and I would be there in just a minute. When I walked into the kitchen, I found two of them standing in front of the gas stove. The had built the sandwich cold, two slices of bread and some cheese, and wrapped it in aluminum foil. As I walked towards them, they were about to put the whole thing on top of a lit burner, no pan.

HAD I NOT WALKED IN WHEN I DID, A PRETTY SUBSTANTIAL STOVE FIRE WAS MAYBE FORTY-FIVE SECONDS AWAY.

When they asked if they could make grilled cheese, I assumed they had observed me, or their mother, doing it properly, and that they knew what they were doing. They of course did not. When I asked why they took the approach that they did, the response was simply, "well, we wanted grilled cheese, but didn't want to wash a pan." Their approach was logical, but ignorant, not to mention dangerous.

In the summer of 1985, I was part of a group of Penfield High School Students who took part in a six-week, exchange student trip to what was then called West Germany. We spent a week in Berlin and then the balance of our time with host families in Düsseldorf.

It was a great trip, and in addition to improving our German language skills we saw all kinds of sights, attended some German school, ate an obscene amount of German food, and spent our Deutschmarks on all kinds of crazy stuff. At that time, the US dollar was very strong against the German Mark, effectively making the whole country about 30% off.

One of my best friends at the time was on the trip with me and we did a good bit of shopping on the streets of Düsseldorf. This friend (let's just call him Tom) was interested in buying a switchblade. Switchblades were illegal in New York, and to a sixteen-year-old boy, it was pretty damn cool.

One day we were in a knife shop and Tom found one he liked. I know now that was he bought was in fact not a switchblade in the purest sense, but something called an "automatic knife."

Tom was not a criminal, nor a violent person. He just wanted to buy something that was legal there and not at home. What teenaged boy wouldn't be tempted to make such a purchase? Tom packed the blade in his checked luggage, and it made it home no problem through the pre-9/11 security of the time.

FAST-FORWARD SEVEN MONTHS.

In March 1986, all of the German students, that had hosted us the previous summer, came to the USA for a reciprocal visit. They landed in New York City and spent a few days there. They then took the train to Rochester where they would live the standard American suburban life for a few weeks. We had planned some trips for our Teutonic guests and one of them was to Niagara Falls.

On the appointed Saturday morning in March, we loaded up a convoy of station wagons, and headed west to cover the seventy miles to the falls. If you are unfamiliar, Niagara Falls can be experienced from both the US and Canada, but the Canadian experience is far superior.

The Canadians have us beat when it comes to the Falls of Niagara

As we were crossing the border, one of the German students presented her passport, but it was not German, it was Hungarian. Since Hungary was still a communist country in 1986, this caused a bit of a problem.

So, as the teachers and border agents sorted out the suspicious "commie," the rest of us went to the park on the New York side of the falls where you can take an elevator down to the edge of the river, downstream from both sets of falls.

SINCE IT WAS MARCH IN UPSTATE NEW YORK, IT WAS STILL WINTER.

Unless you've visited Niagara Falls in the winter (and most people haven't), the river below the falls freezes. In fact there have been times that the falls themselves have frozen, but in March 1986, the falls were free flowing into the "plunge pool." The top of the river was frozen, allowing the flow of the river underneath the ice.

As we stood at the edge of the frozen river, my friend Tom (remember Tom) decided to take a few steps out onto the ice. Despite the fact that it was sunny and the temperature was in the high 40s, the ice seemed stable to Tom, so he kept going.

Tom hopped across the ice, leaping over large cracks and fissures as he went. We all thought he was nuts, but nobody was willing to go out there and stop him.

TOM JUST KEPT GOING.

Here's the problem. In addition to being dangerous, what Tom was doing was getting closer to illegal with every step. The border between the USA and Canada is in the middle of the Niagara River and Tom was damn close to the middle. In fact, before the shrieking border agents and park police made it down to the shoreline, Tom had actually crossed over into Canada.

After a great deal of screaming and jumping up and down, we were able to get Tom's attention and get him to come back to the shore.

In addition to the legal problems with Tom's little adventure, he had put himself in far greater danger than he ever knew was possible. You see the frozen Niagara River is stable – until it isn't. Some time in March every spring, the icepack "lets go" without any warning, turning from a stable ice bridge to a fast-flowing river of little pieces. This happens so quickly that if it had occurred with Tom out there, he would have most likely met with a violent and chilly death.

In fact, on February 4th 1912, the "Great Ice Bridge Disaster" occurred when the ice bridge suddenly broke apart, killing three people.

AFTER TURNING AROUND, TOM FINALLY REACHED THE SHORELINE HE WAS IMMEDIATELY ARRESTED.

Tom's parents were not along on the trip, but my mother was and she was sucked into the unenviable task of accompanying Tom to the Park Police station. As they walked, Tom reached into his pocket, leaned over placing his coiled fist into hers and under his breath said, "put this in your purse."

Now, if you know my mother (and even if you don't) this was a pretty big ask, but not wanting to make a bad situation worse, she complied with his request. It was not drugs or some other horrible contraband; it was of course the illegal German switchblade.

Tom was processed and released into the custody of my mother, who was "beyond words" with the whole situation.

With the both "Tommy" and the "Commie" sorted out, we all finally made it across the border to the Canadian side of the falls and had a fine afternoon before returning home at the end of the day.

FOR THE NEXT FIFTEEN YEARS, EVERY TIME TOM'S MOTHER RAN INTO MY MOTHER THE FIRST WORDS OUT OF HER MOUTH WERE, "SHARON, I'M SORRY."

Tom was not trying to initiate a suicidal, international confrontation any more than my children were trying to cause a bread and cheese house fire. In both cases, they simply didn't know any better.

With the access they have to information, kids today are very sophisticated and they know a lot, but they don't know everything, even though they think they do. What's worse, as parents we often assume they know more than they actually do.

So, the next time your child is about to do something, and they claim to be (or you think they are) fully informed, verify what they know to be true. Before long you'll realize that in some cases they don't have a clue, and you'll both be glad you figured it out before somebody causes an international incident.

This is the week you challenge your assumptions about what you think other people know.

Much like a judge that asks a court reporter to read back a passage from a trial, make a point of asking those with whom you interact, to state their understanding of an assumption you have.

Most of the time all you will be doing is verifying that everything is okay, but keep it up and you will soon encounter a substantial gap in understanding, and that can save you from an unpleasant situation.

Stephen S. Nazarian

39 – BLUFF IN POKER – NOT IN PARENTING

Muhammad Ali is famous for saying, "it ain't bragging if you can back it up." In a way, bragging is no different than bluffing. In both cases you are making a statement that nobody can verify on the spot. If you're good enough, you never have the reveal the truth, but if they call your bluff, well that's a whole other story.

When I was growing up, my Dad had Tuesday afternoons off. Sometimes he would use the time for himself, but most of the time, Tuesday afternoons were for adventures. One Tuesday afternoon, I remember my Dad and brother and I piled into the station wagon seeking adventure. There may have been others in the car, but it was definitely Dad, Doug and me.

We were going for a hike, on a new trail, at a place called the Thousand Acre Swamp. This was our first time going to this place, but we had no, Internet nor GPS. All we could do is head in the general direction of where we'd heard it was.

I think I must have been around eight years old, and that would have made my brother ten. In the back seat of the station wagon we got a little silly. For some reason we had settled into this annoying volley, where one of us would say "rooster," and moments later the other would say "roaster." I have no idea how this came about, but it was definitely rooster and roaster.

As we drove around, my Dad became increasingly frustrated with his inability to find the place we were looking for. At the same time, our parlay of rooster/roaster was escalating in lock-step with my father's frustration.

THIS WAS OF COURSE A PERFECT STORM FOR A PARENTAL EXPLOSION, AND ONCE THE CONDITIONS WERE IDEAL, THERE WAS NO AVOIDING THE INEVITABLE.

My Dad whirled around to the backseat, and firmly proclaimed that if we uttered one more rooster or roaster that we would not be going on the hike.

I don't recall if it was Doug, or me but one of us quietly said "rooster." That was it, my Dad declared the adventure both ruined and over. We went home quietly, all retreating to neutral corners.

Around the same time, maybe a year later, my brother and I got it into our heads that we needed skateboards. My Dad being a pediatrician regularly saw the broken arms and wrists from the skateboarding craze. He stated that he would not be party to any skateboard purchases. If we wanted them, we would need to save up and get them with our own money.

We saved our allowances and lawn mowing money. We tried to have a lemonade stand, but success in such endeavors is elusive to the children of cul-de-sacs.

The Makaha "kicktail," aint she a beauty

In the end, it took a few months, but we finally saved enough. I think it was something like $18 each.

We both decided on the same model: a banana yellow Makaha "kicktail" with green wheels. Let me tell you they were schweet!

One Saturday afternoon only a few weeks later, the girl from next door, who was both older and taller than me, was standing on my skateboard out in the driveway. Since she had a habit of teasing me, I saw an opportunity to score a few points of my own.

I calmly walked over towards my skateboard and asked her to give it back. I knew for certain that she wouldn't, and when she refused I kicked it right out from under her.

Being an awkwardly tall adolescent girl, she flailed a bit, but before falling to the ground she managed to regain her balance; I regained control of my skateboard.

Unfortunately for me, my Dad had seen the whole thing from the garage. Witnessing my complete disregard for the safely of the neighbor girl, he came right out to me, grabbed the skateboard and said, "You will write me a ten sentence essay by Monday morning about why what you just did was such a careless thing, or the garbage man's kid is going to get a great new skateboard."

I couldn't believe it. It was my skateboard, purchased with my money. I was incredulous. I didn't think he'd go through with it, so did not write the essay by Monday morning.

MY SKATEBOARD TOOK A RIDE ON THE GARBAGE TRUCK NEVER TO BE SEEN AGAIN.

On a Sunday morning in the spring of 2014, the parent/child world came full circle. My wife arose early to go to work. At 7:15, I sent the one child who was awake upstairs to roust the other three. At 7:40, I sent a different child to make sure all four were moving and getting ready. This is nothing new, since we normally attend 8:30 Sunday mass, and always leave the house between 8:10 and 8:15 – always.

At 8:05 we were all gathered in the kitchen except for one. I asked the present three where the fourth might be. They all said nothing and looked at each other in that clueless way that only responsibility-dodging siblings can.

I MARCHED UP THE STAIRS TO FIND THE MISSING CHILD STILL ASLEEP IN BED.

I sternly woke the child with my voice and proclaimed, "we are leaving in six minutes, with or without you." It was 8:06.

At 8:13 I was sitting in the car with the other three. We started backing down the driveway fully expecting the fourth to fly out the door at any moment. It never happened. We went to church, minus one child.

My cell phone vibrated at 8:28, I did not answer. The child called Mom at work, several texts were sent, but in the end, the child stayed home and had to ride his bike, alone, to the 11:00am mass at a closer church.

Although I felt justified in my action, I was worried about the child the whole time. And just so you know I'm not a complete ogre, the "child" was plenty old enough to stay home alone. The name and age have been omitted only to protect the guilty.

Generally, our kids are very well behaved. We have high expectations, and for the most part they meet or exceed them. However, children are little humans and are subject to the same temptations of human nature as anyone else. They push boundaries, and they test to see if the actual edges are any different than the stated ones.

It has been said that people remember stories not facts, and that an experience is much more meaningful than information alone. In the realm of discipline, both of these points are indisputable. Of all the punishments I received between birth, and leaving my parent's home, the rooster/roaster and skateboard incidents have stuck with me more than any other.

I CALLED MY FATHER'S BLUFF TWICE AND IT COST ME A HIKE AND A SKATEBOARD.

That sunny Sunday morning I showed all four of our children that their mother and I are to be taken seriously. It was as much of a lesson to the other three as it was to the slugabed who failed to rise and shine.

Like Muhammad Ali, my Dad and I were willing to back it up and you should be too. I can't promise it will help your card game, but it should make your kids easier to deal with, eventually.

This week, make an effort, in everything you do, to be clear, precise and follow through. The fastest way to earn the respect of others is to keep all of your promises, both good and bad. Once they think you might be bluffing you'll never be taken seriously.

At the same time, be on the lookout for the bluffs of others. If someone issues a threat or ultimatum, tell them that you expect them to follow through, win or lose.

---

40 – BINARY, OR NOT?

Have you ever been driving behind a car with a sticker that says "PZEV?" It is a designation issued by the California Air Resources Board (CARB) and it means (I am not making this up):

Partial
Zero
Emissions
Vehicle

Yes that's right. A government agency saw fit to give partial credit to a binary designation. Zero, means zero and by saying something is a partial zero, sort of takes away the power zero had in the first place, right?

Government logic at its best

I'm not talking about the merits of improved vehicle emissions, carbon or climate change, but rather the accuracy of things, and knowing when it makes sense to use a binary designation versus one with more granularity.

It has often been said that you can't be "a little pregnant." This is absolutely true. Pregnancy is a binary condition, either you are or you're not. You can be unsure of your condition, but once the data is collected, there are only two possible answers.

When I was in high school, report card grades were given as letters (ABCD) enhanced with plusses and minuses. The ranges, take B for example, were like this:

80%-82% = B-

83%-86% = B

87%-89% = B+

Of course any grade received on a report card, was inevitably argued by the recipient, to be at the very top edge of the range.

To combat this "wiggle room," some time between my graduation and my oldest child entering 6th grade in the same school district, they adopted a straight percentage on report cards to replace letter grades. What's funny is that the argument has now shifted to tenths of a percentage. Would adding tenths to the report card end this argument once and for all?   When binary isn't an option, how much granularity is enough?

In college some classes were offered as "pass-fail." There was no question as to how you did, though I suppose those who failed could argue that they "just missed it."

In 1986, Michael Keaton starred in a movie called *Gung Ho*. The basic plot was that a Japanese car company purchased a defunct American factory to make their cars stateside. It was entertaining to watch the American workers clash with Japanese management and work philosophy, but there was a scene about three quarters into the movie that has stuck with me for almost thirty years.

The American workers had been promised a bonus if they could achieve a specific production goal. They accepted the challenge, but when it looked like they wouldn't make it, they came back to management and asked, "what about half the bonus for half the goal?"

They had been given a binary condition (achievement = bonus) and they accepted it. When it looked like they were going to lose, they wanted more granularity, more options. As you might imagine, management was not open to the idea.

This scene replays in my mind often when I am having similar parenting moments with my children, or management moments at work. There seems to be this idea that everything can be broken down into finer slices, no matter what the agreement was at the outset.

IF IT LOOKS LIKE YOU MIGHT LOSE – RENEGOTIATE.

In the 1975 release of *One Flew Over the Cuckoo's Nest*, there is a scene where the residents of a mental institution are playing cards, and using cigarettes as currency.

A cigarette in the game is equal to a dime. One player tries to bet two half cigarettes as a dime and the character played by Jack Nicholson colorfully explains why two halves do not equal a whole.

The smallest acceptable level of granularity was one whole cigarette, and this guy learned that the hard way.

═══════════════════════

As the machines in our lives have made the transition from analog to digital, we have enjoyed the benefit of binary over granular in lots of ways. Remember when televisions and radios had "fine tuning" knobs? We don't have to fine-tune anything anymore, we just punch in the station and it is there, on, tuned in, rock solid.

In other parts of our digital lifestyle, binary has taken a little longer to be as good as analog. Look at the screens on smartphones. I have an original iPhone that my kids still use to play games on long car trips. If I look at that screen today, I can see every square pixel.

At the time it came out, it was state of the art, but in the years since, screens have improved to the point where the pixels are small enough that my eye can't distinguish one from the next. The digital is now so smooth that it looks to my eye like analog. Apple figured out and achieved the right level of granularity.

In business, parenting, and life in general we all strive to hit the mark as accurately as we can. Sometimes this is easy and at other times it can be nearly impossible.

> *REFEREES USE A COIN TOSS TO START GAMES BECAUSE THERE IS NO AMBIGUITY AS TO THE OUTCOME; IT IS EITHER HEADS OR TAILS — PERIOD.*

Unfortunately, most of life isn't that simple, the trick is in figuring just the right amount of granularity for a given situation. There is no formula for doing this, only experience, trial and error.

I guess the thing that bothers me still about the scene in *Gung Ho* is that society is stuck on the idea that failure is bad. Sure, it isn't what we're going for, but I have learned more from my failures than my successes, and I can say confidently that many of those successes were due to what I first learned by failing.

When the last place U9 soccer team still goes home with a trophy, it robs them of the growth that comes with losing, while at the same time it dilutes the victory of the first place team.

> **JUST BECAUSE YOU CAN ADD MORE GRANULARITY TO A SITUATION DOESN'T MEAN THAT YOU SHOULD.**

If you can manage a situation with a binary condition, good for you, but if you need to get more specific, try to keep it chunky enough to know what went right and what went wrong.

I may never understand the logic that produced the "partial zero" designation, but I can tell you this – if I every got one on a report card I'd be hard pressed to talk my way out of it.

As you go about your business, take an extra moment this week to analyze if the level of granularity you are giving or receiving is right for the situation.

You may find that a slight adjustment will make huge difference. You might also uncover places where you are simply doing more work than is necessary.

Try and reduce things to the smallest level of specificity that will work. You might overcorrect and have to backpedal a bit, but the exercise will be both enlightening and satisfying.

I promise a result that is equal to or greater than a "partial zero" which is of course more than nothing.

---

41 – THE LOGIC OF INSPIRING GREATNESS

When our four children were younger, we used to encourage good behavior at church on Sunday morning by issuing a standard, age-weighted "grade" after each service. If the average across all four of them ended up being a "B" or better, then they would be rewarded with a dozen donuts. If the average was a B- or lower, then they got bupkis, nada, zilch. There was no "half-dozen for a C" option.

As we all know (well most of us anyway) one really bad grade can ruin an average; so one bad apple could kill the donut potential for the bushel of them.

FOR A FEW YEARS THIS APPROACH WORKED WELL, BUT THEN A FUNNY THING HAPPENED.

Without warning, we passed a turning point. In the evil little minds of our four children, the pleasure of being the cause of another's bad grade had ascended to a point above that of a fresh Boston cream, or a French cruller. Or in other words, they'd rather see their siblings suffer than enjoy the spoils of good behavior.

The four Nazarian children, showing their best "pouty" faces

All of this was happening in church no less.

Emily and I were flummoxed. Even though I am the middle of three and my bride the eleventh of twelve, neither of us saw this coming. We didn't know what to do, because the very basis of their approach was foreign to us both.

IT WAS THE KID EQUIVALENT OF A SUICIDE BOMBER OR KAMIKAZE PILOT.

After a few weeks of coming to the realization that this paradigm was real, and probably permanent, we sat down one Sunday afternoon to devise a new approach.

The bottom line was, we wanted our children to be well behaved in church. We knew that they were inclined not to be, and three of them being boys, made it all the worse. We needed a clever plan and fast. We knew they could do it, because they'd shown us that they could, but kids today are pretty sophisticated, so our approach was going to have to be equally refined.

As we discussed our options, we noted a trend we had seen recently and we thought we just might be able to us it to our advantage.

A few times in recent months, and mostly when visiting other churches, we (and by that I mean the kids) had received a completely unsolicited, behavioral complement from a total stranger. We had used these as data towards the grade, but what if...

WHAT IF WE USED IT AS THE TOTAL MEASURE?
AND SO IT WAS – GENIUS!

From that day forward donuts would only be offered if we, as a family, received an unsolicited complement from some random churchgoer.

In a way it was a perfect response to their desire to sabotage each other, since the only way to even approach success was to collectively perform so well as to be noticed by someone who should actually be paying attention to something else.

No longer was there any joy in subverting the behavior of a single sibling, since the very concept of the individual in the equation had been eliminated. The idea of Charlotte, Lewis, Oliver and Lawrence was no longer – there was only the collective. It may sound a little Marxist, but it was four against two – war is hell.

What was worse (for them) was that a perfect performance didn't guarantee success. It only created the conditions for success. They were completely beholden to the notice of those around them.

Or in the words of Blanche DuBois, they had no choice but to:

"RELY ON THE KINDNESS OF STRANGERS."

Well, it worked; and it worked really well. Somehow they now manage to pull off the unsolicited complement almost every week, even though we attend the same mass with the same basic crowd. However, their batting average for churches away from home is a perfect 1,000.

I've used a similar technique when leading software developers. From time to time a customer will ask for something that has never been done before. Generally we know what they are asking for is possible, but we have no idea how possible or exactly how to execute. So, instead of demanding that the programmers figure it out, I tell them that the customer doesn't think it can be done. With this approach, I've never had to disappoint a customer.

The concept here is counter-intuitive, but effective. By setting the expectations high, but the measure of success as limitless, those being charged have no choice but to give it everything they have. The best part is that if success is not achieved, they only blame themselves, not you.

IN SETTING EXPECTATIONS, IT IS OKAY TO MARK THE FLOOR, BUT BE CAREFUL TO NEVER DEFINE A CEILING.

We really have no idea what others are capable of, and we should be careful never to limit them by that lack of understanding.

In this age of children (of all ages) expecting a predictable, and reliable result for their efforts, it is nice to see people achieve untold greatness based on their unlimited potential, not just on what they think they need to do, to get what they "deserve."

In programming terms, the goal is to replace the IF-THEN statement with a WHAT-IF attitude. Look around you. You'll find plenty of places to apply this. And if you see my kids in church, I'm certain they will toss you a jelly-filled for a single, well-placed, complement.

Are you holding back those you lead (children, employees, dogs, etc.) by putting a limit on what you expect?

When setting expectations, look critically at what you say, and how you say it. Every time you issue a charge this week, make sure your audience knows the minimum expectations, but be clear that there is no limit on what they can actually deliver. The results will likely surprise you.

Stephen S. Nazarian

42 – MAKING DO WITH CLASSIC ROCK

Do you ever find yourself stuck because you don't have the resources you think you need to move forward? The philosophical shift you're looking for is as close as the local classic rock station.

"AND IF YOU CAN'T BE WITH THE ONE YOU LOVE HONEY, LOVE THE ONE YOU'RE WITH"

-Stephen Stills

Years ago, before GPS and Google Earth, we used to travel from place to place using these large folded pieces of paper called maps.

Typically when you were traveling to see someone, you would follow the map to his or her town, and then you'd follow the directions given to you by the person you were visiting. Of course these were directions given over the phone, and scribbled on the back of an envelope or a scrap of paper. There was no texting, no email, it was far from a perfect system but it was all we had.

When my wife and I got married in 1999 (yes, we did party like it was... well, because it was) the glovebox in her car was stuffed with these relics of pre-smartphone navigation. I think we finally threw them away in 2007.

I AM NOT A TERRIBLY DETAIL-ORIENTED PERSON, AND I HAVE AWFUL HANDWRITING, SO I DIDN'T DO WELL WITH THE PRE-INTERNET "LAST MILE" DIRECTIONS SYSTEM.

Because of this I developed a little system of my own that worked until they invented Mapquest and the Tom-Tom. When the map ran out of detail and I found myself in the town where I was headed, I would drive around until I found a pizzeria with a "we deliver" sign out front.

Having been a pizza delivery boy in high school I knew that such places have detailed local maps on the wall. I would walk into the pizza joint with the address I was looking for, and ask them how to get there. A few minutes later I would be on my way to my final destination, no awkward call from a payphone necessary. Most people didn't recognize a pizzeria for the navigational resource that it was.

_____

When I was a kid, we vacationed in the Adirondacks for several years in a row. Every year we went, my dad would pick out a mountain for us to climb. The rules were simple: no whining, there will be many educational opportunities along the hike, and finally,

WE DO NOT EAT LUNCH UNTIL WE GET TO THE TOP OF THE MOUNTAIN.

One year we climbed our mountain, and as we sat and eating our lunch, my dad was giving a geology lesson. He pointed out some of the details of the rocks on which we were sitting, and that some of it was quartz.

My older brother who is a bit of a skeptic (he's a lawyer now, a judge in fact) asked my dad how he knew it was quartz. My dad thought a minute and then went into the remnants of our lunch bag. He found the baggie that had held some dill pickles and said "if I'm right, quartz will bubble and foam in the presence of acid, like this pickle juice." He then poured the pickle juice on the quartz.

Well, my brother was skeptical no more and my sister and I were speechless.

_____

A few years after college, I was helping a friend and his roommate move into a new apartment. After a day of lugging furniture up three flights of stairs we ordered a pizza, devouring it in minutes.

His roommate's mother was there for the last part of the move and she asked what we were going to do for dessert. The three of us laughed since we knew very little food had been moved from their previous apartment and it was too late to go get anything.

In the fridge were seven eggs and some milk. On the counter were salt, pepper and sugar. The roommate's mom looked at what there was, scratched her head and told us to go continue unpacking.

Thirty minutes later she appeared with four coffee mugs. In each was about an inch of sweet custard that she has made in the oven from the eggs, sugar and the milk.

SO OFTEN WE FIND OURSELVES IN SITUATIONS WHERE WE THINK WE NEED ADDITIONAL RESOURCES, BUT IF WE LOOK MORE CLOSELY AT WHAT WE ALREADY HAVE AVAILABLE TO US, WE SOMETIMES FIND THAT WE HAVE EVERYTHING WE NEED.

So, the next time you hear yourself saying, "I can't [whatever] because I don't have [whatever else]" take a moment, look around, and find a pizzeria, some pickle juice or some custard fixings'. You may not have exactly what you'd like, but you just might find you have what you need.

"YOU CAN'T ALWAYS GET WHAT YOU WANT BUT IF YOU TRY SOMETIMES, WELL YOU JUST MIGHT FIND YOU GET WHAT YOU NEED"

-The Rolling Stones

How clever or creative do you push yourself to be? When faced with an obstacle, do you shut down and give up, or do you circle the wagons and look for a way through.

For the next week, look for instances where you are about to accept defeat. In every case, refuse and take whatever time you need to find a way over the hurdle with the resources you have available to you.

Your approach might not be perfect, but in most cases done beats perfect. Those perfect people are annoying anyway, right?

Stephen S. Nazarian

43 – What Happened Next, I Did Not See Coming

We all know the popular expression, "you can't please all the people, all of the time." As true as this is, it is often said with the subtext that if it were in fact possible, pleasing all of the people all of the time would be a good thing. I am here to tell you that it wouldn't be, at least not the way most people think of it.

When I was in the tenth grade, I was still trying to hold onto my lifelong affinity for singing while maintaining my more recently developed love of running. Although things today are even more intense for the average high-schooler, back in the 1980s, keeping commitments to music and athletics at the same time was a scheduling quagmire few opted to tackle.

In my situation, I was heading into my fourth year of cross-country, and for the first time in my life, I was actually succeeding at an athletic endeavor. I was also about to start my second year as a member of the Penfield High School Jazz Choir. Having been selected

PHS Jazz Choir spring 1984 - I said I enjoyed the music and the people. I didn't say anything about the uniform

to be a member of this elite group as a freshman was an honor, and I enjoyed both the music and the people.

I was doing a decent job of juggling the two schedules, often showing up to choir rehearsal in my running attire, and sometimes having to run through the finish at a cross country meet, and jump into the car where I would change on the way to a choir performance. It was crazy, but doable because I was 15, and because my parents were very supportive of it all.

Like any system that is already operating at the margins, all it takes is one additional variable to take the situation from managed chaos to complete cataclysm. In the fall of 1984, the variable came in the form of:

- A parents' weekend visit to see my brother who was a freshman at Yale
- A rare Saturday event for the Jazz Choir – a 24-hour fundraising dance marathon

I had the parents' weekend thing pretty well worked out since the cross-country coach was flexible about missing one Saturday meet per season for a family or other important obligation.

Let me say for the record; even way back then, missing one extracurricular activity for another was frowned upon by the leader of the activity you were missing. This was way before commitment contracts and other such things, but it was an unwritten rule that if you committed to something you were committing to it fully. Or said another way, the XC coach didn't mind that you were in Jazz Choir, so long as you never missed XC for JC. The Jazz Choir director felt the same way.

SO, YOU CAN SEE THE DANGEROUS GAME I HAD CHOSEN TO PLAY.

As I sat and contemplated my fate, it seemed like there was no answer to my conundrum. On the first Saturday in question, were both a very important XC meet and the dance marathon. The following Saturday was a less important meet, but also parent's weekend.

WHAT WAS A SKINNY, OVERCOMMITTED TENTH-GRADER TO DO?

While out mowing the lawn on a Sunday afternoon, I had a flash of brilliance. On the first Saturday, I would attend the dance marathon and use up my one XC meet "miss." The next weekend I would stay home from parent's weekend and attend my XC meet. I ran inside, called my friend Andy to see if I could stay with his family while may parents were away. His parents said that would be fine and I thought I had figured out how to please everyone.

The aforementioned skinny, overcommitted tenth-grader

Later that evening I presented my plan to my parents, expecting to be recognized for both my cleverness, and my willingness to sacrifice parents' weekend for peace in the world of Penfield High School extra curriculars.

WHAT HAPPENED NEXT, I DID NOT SEE COMING.

My Dad listened to my plan and calmly asked two questions: "Do you want to go to parents' weekend?" I replied "yes, but…"

He continued, "if I drove you, how much dance marathon would you miss to go run your race and get right back?"

I thought about it for a minute and said, "about an hour and a half." My father then looked me right in the eye and said, "I understand where you are coming from, but you are trading parents' weekend for 90 minutes of dancing, does that sound like a good deal?"

Of course he was right. What I failed to recognize was that although not ideal, in the eyes of the Choir Director, twenty-two and a half hours of dancing was enough to keep her happy.

MY SOPHOMORIC BRAIN HAD DECIDED THAT KEEPING EACH LEADER IN MY WORLD HAPPY WAS AN ALL-OR-NOTHING PROPOSITION. OF COURSE IT WAS NOT.

A quarter-century later, I had a customer for whom my company annually manufactured several million units of a product that they sold in each of their 6,000+ stores. Their inventory system was fully automated, so when stock would get low, automatic orders would appear for us to fill. Unfortunately "fully-automated" does not mean foolproof, and every so often the system would hiccup. When this happened I would get a panicked call from the customer telling me that they needed 400,000 pieces… tomorrow!

What they were actually saying was; "if our system had worked properly, we would have placed an order ten days ago and we'd have 400,000 pieces in our now almost empty warehouses by now."

This was our largest customer, and many companies would have dropped everything to give them what they were asking for, however my father had taught me to let cooler heads prevail and find a smarter solution. Furthermore, we physically did not have the capability to make 400,000 pieces in a day – the best we could do was about 50,000. So, when this would happen, I would ask the customer to take a breath and tell me where the situation was the worst, and one distribution center at a time (they had thirteen) we would go down the list making a plan for keeping the product flowing without interruption.

Human beings are funny creatures. We all have a twisted love/hate relationship with crisis. At all costs we seek to avoid them, but at the same time most of us get a real charge out of triumphing over one. This disconnected thinking comes from the fact that most crises are much less dire (or binary) then they seem at the outset. Taking the time to dissect the details, and create a calm and logical approach to the situation will always produce a better result for everyone.

In fact, after a few of these panicked situations with the customer they stopped calling in a fright and instead called to say, "our inventory system screwed up again, how can we keep the product flowing?"

I need to backpedal a little on my opening paragraph. I said that pleasing all the people all the time is both impossible and undesirable. I would now like to say that pleasing all the people all the time is possible, but not with what they ask for the first time.

COMMUNICATION IS THE KEY.

Don't ever be afraid to respond to a request with what you can do, as opposed to what was requested. Chances are, what you can do, will be more than enough. After all if they could do it themselves they wouldn't have called in the first place, right?

How often to people come to you in a frenzied panic? Do you meet their panic with more panic or calm? This week, every time somebody is flipping out about something, calmly grab a piece of paper and a pencil. Ask the person flipping out for all the information they have and calmly diagram the problem. Look at it together and figure out how to address it in a logical and cool manner. That is something I promise they will never expect.

44 – PAY NO ATTENTION TO THE MAN BEHIND THE COUNTER

In January 2014, my company sent me to the International Consumer Electronics show (CES) in Las Vegas. I've done my fair share of work in Vegas, but I'd never been to CES and I was excited to go. We would be exhibiting my company's educational video games in an emerging technology area called Eureka Park.

The tradeshow team would be made up of me, Emma our marketing coordinator, and a sales helper from the west coast who would meet us at the show. As the day of departure drew closer, we gathered up all of our material and tradeshow supplies. We had purchased something called a "Turn-key booth" so we only needed to bring a small amount of stuff with us. We were flying Southwest, so our tradeshow material was going to be the second free bag for both of us.

NO NEED TO SHIP ANYTHING.

We had been invited to exhibit by the National Science Foundation, through which we were working on a grant. The program coordinator had given us VERY specific instructions that stated we needed to be present to claim our booth space by 2:00pm on Monday January 6th. The show started Tuesday morning. If we were not there by 2:00pm on Monday, our booth space would be forfeited.

There was an early Monday morning flight that would get us to Vegas by late morning, but I didn't want to risk it, so Emma and I booked a 5:40pm flight on Sunday the 5th that connected through Chicago Midway.

One of the many "Nazarian rules of travel" is:

NEVER CONNECT THROUGH CHICAGO IN THE WINTER.

I was reluctant to break this rule, but when we were booking flights the economics really gave us no choice.

The previous week had brought a big messy snowstorm to the Northeast, but as the weekend approached it looked like things would be fine. I picked up Emma at 3:00pm and we headed to the office to do a final check, and to grab all of the tradeshow bits. We made quick work of the organizing, and as we climbed aboard the parking shuttle my watch read 3:58, plenty of time.

The first sign that things might be a tad messy came from the shuttle driver who asked us, "what airline?" When we responded "Southwest," he just laughed and said, "I doubt it. I've been bringing Southwest passengers back to their cars for the last two hours." Emma and I shot each other a concerned glance, then a shrug, and off we went.

Since we were checking bags, we had to stand in the longer-than-normal line at the counter. As we patiently advanced, we saw that most people were being told bad news about their travel plans because of another snowstorm in the Midwest.

When it was our turn, the gentleman behind the counter looked our itinerary and said, "Your plane leaving Rochester is delayed and you're not going to make your connection in Chicago. Looking at what I have available, I can maybe get you to Vegas on Thursday, but you're going nowhere tonight." I asked about flights out of Chicago on Monday and his response was as immediate as it was terse, "they're all full, not gonna happen."

EMMA AND I STEPPED AWAY FROM THE COUNTER TO REGROUP.

Now, I'm a pretty optimistic guy, but when you're at the mercy of the airlines, your optimism and $6 will buy you a bottle of water at Hudson News.

Emma and I sat down and discussed our options. First I asked my iPhone, "hey Siri, how long it would take to drive to Las Vegas?" She replied in her unfeeling tone, "thirty-seven hours," ouch!

WE ENTERTAINED CAPITULATING TO THE ABRUPT "SOUTHWEST GUY" BUT IN THE END THAT ONLY GUARANTEED THE RESULT WE WERE TRYING TO AVOID – NOT GETTING TO CES.

We decided we simply needed get on that plane. None of the planes going to Las Vegas were in Rochester they were all in Chicago. We also further surmised that even though all the flights to Vegas on Monday were supposedly sold out, the majority of those seats were held by passengers who were ALSO NOT GETTING TO CHICAGO!

As we stood in line again, I called the Southwest toll-free number and spoke with a nice lady who told me that if I was confirmed on the flight to

Chicago, the attendant in Rochester couldn't prevent me from boarding, but if I did, I would give up my chance at a refund.

BY NOT GETTING TO CES, WE STOOD TO LOSE A WHOLE LOT MORE MONEY THAN THAT.

So, when we got to the front of the line, we had to let two other people go by so we could avoid the previous guy and talk with a different counter agent. We stated our case, checked the bags and headed to the gate.

The original 5:40 flight had been delayed three times already and was now scheduled for 7:15. When we finally boarded and began to taxi, it was nearly 8:00pm.

Emma and I had downloaded some flight tracking apps to our phones and as we were being told to shut our phones off, it looked like we would miss our connection in Chicago by 20 minutes. My favorite is FlightAware's Flight Tracker, because it gets all its data from the FAA.

HOW BAD ARE THE AIRLINES AT TELLING YOU THE TRUTH, WHEN THE BETTER DATA COMES FROM THE FEDERAL GOVERNMENT?

As we took to the air, we said many prayers asking the Gods of aviation to delay the Vegas flight just enough so that we would make it.

As we touched down at Midway, we fired up our phones to see how we had fared. Our bet had paid off – big time.

The connecting flight was still on the ground, was beginning to board and was only two gates away. We walked off our first flight, strolled the 50 yards to the departure gate and literally walked right onto the Vegas flight never breaking stride. Of course once on that plane, we sat for more than an hour before taking off. We later learned that our flight out was the very last one to leave Midway before they closed the airport.

We got to Vegas at 1:00am pacific time (4:00am east coast body time), but we got there. Our bags didn't show up until Wednesday afternoon, but that circus of resourcefulness is entertaining enough for another chapter all by itself.

The lesson here is simple: in the face of unexpected adversity, fully think through all of your options and gather as much data as you possibly can. Most of the people in line with us the first time through simply accepted what the airline told them and went home.

I knew that there was a chance I was going to sleep on the floor in Chicago, but in the end I spent the night in a comfy bed on the Vegas strip.

Emma, manning the booth in Eureka Park

Never be afraid to challenge assumptions; don't always accept what you're told, and make decisions based on data, not what the guy behind the counter tells you. Certainly there was some gambling and luck involved that night, but we were heading to Las Vegas after all.

We are all presented with chance, odds and gambling in situations every day. All you can do is gather enough information to keep the odds ever in your favor.

For the coming week, do not accept anything at face value. I'm not telling you to be cynical, bur rather hyper-analytical. Most of the time the person from whom you receive the information is simply doing their job, but don't let that lull you into complacency. Pick apart the information you have until you've figured out a way to get what you need. You might end up spending a night on the floor of an airport, but you will eventually reach you destination.

45 – HOW TO FIX A FAUCET WITH A SINK

In my senior year of college I took a playwriting course. I figured we'd read a lot of plays, study them and perhaps write a scene or two of our own. The class was being taught by a playwright-in-residence, and on the first day of class he proclaimed:

"I know you all know how read and discuss dramatic literature, you wouldn't be here if you didn't, so this semester you are going to write a play. No, not together, each of you will write your own one-act play. That's the class, so get up and walk out now if you can't handle it."

IT WAS NOT WHAT I HAD EXPECTED, BUT I DID NOT WALK OUT.

Over the course of the semester I did write my own one-act play. It was called *Bunkbeds* and it was about two college freshman roommates. It had five scenes. It had a proper beginning, middle, and an end. It followed all the formulas and processes we had been taught. On paper it was finished, but I had a nagging feeling that it was missing something – something really important. I scoured my text, I edited, I read, I re-read and I edited again, but I couldn't figure out how to fix it… until.

It was the night before the play was due. I had been ready to turn it in for more than a week, but that feeling had kept me from doing so. I was sleeping soundly (ironically) in my own bunk bed when I popped awake with the answer.

The five scenes of the play took place across the first semester of the characters' freshman year, but what it needed was some perspective. I got out of bed, turned on my Macintosh SE, with the 9" black & white screen, and wrote both a prologue and epilogue given by the main character on his college graduation day. The prologue took place before the ceremony and the epilogue just after. It was exactly what the play was missing.

SO WHAT DOES ANY OF THIS HAVE TO DO WITH A FAUCET AND A SINK?
HAVE FAITH AND READ ON.

We moved into our current house in 2002, but it was built in 1971. The two upstairs bathrooms were still "original" and if you Google 1970s bathroom decoration you will get a sense of what we had signed up for.

The kid's bathroom is quite large with two sinks set in a long counter. From day one, the faucets leaked. I know my way around faucet repair, but these bad boys were something else. They were really odd, slanted numbers that were compatible only with the equally odd slanted sinks into which they were installed.

Little by little I replaced everything, washers, packing, seats and stems. No matter what I did, they still leaked, and worse so when the not-so-strong hands of our three young children were responsible for shutting them off.

The evil Eljer slanted faucets

I would have loved to just go down to Home Depot and pick up two $35 faucets and be done with it, but the crazy slanted mounting holes of the sink made that impossible. I searched near and far for new faucets that would work, but nobody had them. Nobody.

One day I drove by the remnants of a torn-out bathroom at the end of a driveway in my neighborhood and looking at the two sinks in the trashed counter I thought; "what if I could find replacement sinks for cheap (or even free), then I could go get those $35 faucets and the problem would be solved.

I started looking for used sinks on Craigslist. There were plenty of folks selling one sink, but nobody selling two.

ONE DAY I NEGLECTED TO PUT THE WORD 'USED' IN MY SEARCH AND I HIT THE JACKPOT.

A guy was selling a brand new, white, American Standard, oval bathroom sink. As I read the listing my internal monologue was saying, "damn, I wish he had two of them" and I nearly squealed with delight as I saw the last line of the posting, which was, "I have two of them, but only one is in a box." Bingo!

The best part was that he was asking only $12 each. That is not a typo, twelve dollars for a brand new bathroom sink. I immediately dropped everything I was doing, called the guy, went to the ATM and drove the 3 miles to his house. By day's end the sinks and new faucets were installed and there hasn't been a leak since.

So what do these two stories have to do with each other? Simple, in both cases the solution I needed was not what I was originally looking for. I thought I knew what I needed and I was wrong.

The new sinks and faucets; the avocado tile is still there from 1971

I have held several sales roles on my career and when I get a call from someone asking for something specific, I always receive that information politely and then ask, "but what are you trying to do?"

AT ANY GIVEN TIME WE ONLY KNOW WHAT WE KNOW, AND IN TURN WE TEND TO ONLY ASK FOR WHAT WE KNOW. BUT, WHAT IF THE BEST SOLUTION IS SOMETHING WE DON'T KNOW?

So, keep an open mind in all things. Ask friends and colleagues for their input when you feel stuck, and don't be afraid to challenge your own assumptions. Learning something new and better does not mean you were wrong; all it means is that you are now smarter.

The first challenge you face this week, for which you think you know the best approach, stop. Take a long, hard look at what you are trying to accomplish and then take a wider view on all of the possible things you could do to get there.

Many of the options you come up with will be horrible.

When you have exhausted every possible avenue, you may end up with the very same plan with which you started. If you do, it will be a far more informed decision, however if you come up with something unexpected, you will have arrived at a level of sophistication in problem solving that most never achieve.

You can then feel free to wash your original idea down the drain of the nearest 1970's era bathroom sink.

46 – Don't Fight The Power

KIDS, CASH, VACATIONS, AND HOW TO NEVER HAVE TO SAY "NO" IN A SOUVENIR SHOP – EVER AGAIN.

In October 2010, we went to Disney World. From the time they were old enough to ask, we had told our children the following about Disney:

- We will go once
- We will do it right
- There will be no napping
- We will not be bringing a stroller

When we finally pulled the trigger, the kids were 10, 9, 8 and 6. We purchased the vacation package in March of that same year, spending the following months planning out how we would spend our nine days in the "Land of the Mouse."

There are endless resources about how to "do Disney" so this story isn't about any of that. This is about a technique you can use with kids on any vacation from a simple overnight to three weeks in Europe.

One day I was reading articles about kids and money at Rachel Cruze's website (www.rachelcruze.com), and I was reminded of a little trick my wife and I came up with, that turned a normally awful part of vacationing with children into an absolute pleasure for us, as well as an education for them.

Rachel Cruze describes herself as a speaker and author on life and money for the next generation. She is the daughter of Dave Ramsey, the noted advisor and radio personality on all things financial. Her website is full of really useful information for families of all kinds. I highly recommend you check it out.

In the summer preceding our trip, we created a program for our kids called "Mommy Bucks." The concept was pretty simple. A Mommy Buck was worth ten cents. Every chore, good deed, or thing of value perpetrated by our children had the potential to earn Mommy Bucks. There was a notebook in the kitchen junk drawer where we kept track of their earnings.

Every once in a while, we would issue a "doubling event." This would come in the form of a room-cleaning contest, or a garden that needed weeding. The winners of these events would see their balance instantly doubled.

Mommy Bucks could be cashed in at any time for spendable cash, but every time they wanted to do so, we would remind them that a doubling event could be just around the corner and anything they took out would lose out on the doubling.

THE ALLURE OF FREE MONEY WAS STRONG, EVEN FOR A SIX-YEAR-OLD.

By the time the summer ended and we were only a month away from our trip, the kids had built up some pretty nice balances in their Mommy Buck accounts. My oldest had more than $100, while the youngest had north of $50. From the beginning, we were very clear with the kids that this trip was a privilege.

IT CERTAINLY WAS THE MOST EXPENSIVE TRIP I'D EVER TAKEN, AND AFTER ALL WAS SAID AND DONE IT COST MORE THAN MY FIRST NEW CAR.

So they knew that everything we were doing had cost money, and we expected that fact to be understood and respected.

Having chosen to purchase the Disney meal plan, and several other inclusive options, we also made sure that the kids understood the difference between "free" and "included."

NOTHING IS FREE, ESPECIALLY AT DISNEY.

For each of the kids I made a little note on my iPhone that held their Mommy Bucks balance. Every time they wanted to buy something, they would come to Emily, or me and we would discuss with them the merits of what they wanted to buy, check their balance, and then they would make the final decision on the purchase.

It was amazing to see all four kids weigh the pros and cons of something as silly as an inflatable sword. Instead of my six-year-old asking me "Daaaad, can I get that sword?" he said something more like, "Dad, you think $12 is a good deal for that sword?" Most of the time I held my tongue on questions of judgment – there are no good deals at Disney.

After each purchase, I noted on my phone what they bought, how much it cost and I calculated a new balance. Every time they came back for more I would simply show them the list of purchases they had chosen and the balance remaining.

WATCHING THEIR LITTLE BRAINS PROCESS ALL THE PREVIOUS DECISIONS, AND WHAT THEY MEANT IN THE PRESENT, WAS ABSOLUTELY FASCINATING.

After a few days of watching our children take ownership of their money and complete responsibility for their purchases, we noticed something. We had not told a child "no," not even once, for anything.

One quick little Disney tip. All Disney hotels will sell you an endlessly refillable cup for something like $18. For your entire trip, at the hotel (not in the parks), you can fill it with coffee in the morning, and soft drinks by the pool in the afternoon. We bought two of these and they served the grownups and the kids alike. It is hot in Orlando and kids are going to want many drinks – we chose to invest $36 in not fighting it. Again, we never had to say no.

If you add it up, my wife and I each have more than half a century parenting years under our respective belts so far.

IF YOU ASKED ME FOR THE ONE THING THAT KIDS TRY TO DO MOST OFTEN, I WOULD NOT HESITATE TO TELL YOU IT IS THIS – OBTAIN POWER.

From the moment the two-day-old infant figures out that enough crying will get him picked-up and held, they try everything they can think of to shift power away from you and to them. Of course the natural reaction is to fight this grab at your parental prerogatives, but we learned at Disney that the opposite could work even better.

By handing all the power over to them, they had to deal with it. The great part was that they learned pretty quickly that getting the power isn't anywhere near as easy as they thought it would be. All four came home with carefully chosen purchases that they owned, completely.

Sure there were some regrets, but nothing horrible and as we adults know all too well, every regret comes with free knowledge for future use.

Every one of them also came home with money to spare. As the trip wound down, they all realized that there was in fact going to be life after Disney, and they all decided that a little cash on hand might be good for reentry into reality.

The Nazarian boys posing with "Ratatouille" souvenirs they chose not to purchase

The 1980's Hip-Hop act, Public Enemy told us that we should FIGHT THE POWER. I'm here to tell you to let them have it. If you do, they can't blame you when the $12 inflatable sword springs a leak, just sayin'.

Look out for power grabbers this week. They might be your kids, your coworkers, or even family members. When you identify someone trying to obtain power or control, reverse your urge to fight it and instead hand it over with grace and encouragement.

First off you will notice that the one looking to obtain the power might just change their mind, but don't stop there. Give them enough rope to get the job done (or hang themselves).

If you do it right, you will have transferred power in a responsible and meaningful way. Additionally, the more you do this, the less you will find you need to do it. Fight the power? Hell no, let 'em have it.

---

47 – TRANSFER STUDENT

The Rochester Marathon is run every September, and for as long as I can remember the Penfield cross-country team has sponsored a water station somewhere along the course. 2014 was no exception and my daughter Charlotte had me drop her off early on a Sunday morning with her teammates to set up.

Several hours later I received a text indicating that it was time to pick her up. In the intervening hours, they had closed many streets to accommodate the runners.

AS I TRIED TO GO BACK THE WAY I CAME, POLICE BARRICADES REPEATEDLY TURNED ME AWAY.

I drove in circles trying to find a way in to where the team was waiting, and I ended up stuck behind the slowest, oldest, Buick-driving, white-haired lady ever. A light would turn green, and she would notice just in time to slowly pull ahead and leave me with the red. Of course at the next light I caught up, but the madness continued for several intersections.

Finally, we both pulled up to a corner where I had an opportunity to get around her. I punched the gas, but as I blew by her sluggish passenger door, I heard a noise.

A LOUD AND VIBRATING CLACK-CLACK-CLACK-CLACK CAME FROM THE BOWELS OF MY CAR, SHAKING BOTH THE VEHICLE, AND THE CONFIDENCE I'VE ENJOYED FOR THE SIX YEARS THAT I'VE OWNED IT.

I let up on the gas and the noise went away, but not the worry borne from what I had just experienced. I found my way to Charlotte and we drove home, taking our time, conservatively pulling away from every stop. When we got home, we tried to recreate the noise by stomping on the gas from a dead stop on our quiet, flat suburban street.

I was hoping it might have been some kind of anomaly, but moments into the experiment my worst fears were confirmed.

SOMETHING WAS SERIOUSLY BROKEN IN MY CAR.

After a little research I determined that the problem was something called the transfer case. The transfer case is the key component that turns a two-wheel drive car into an all-wheel drive car. In simple terms, the Transfer Case takes power heading to the two main drive wheels and shares it with the other two wheels.

Mechanically, it is a very simple part. In fact, it is little more than a very robust single-speed bicycle, made up of two shafts, two gears and a chain. Well, it is a little more complex than that, but you get the idea.

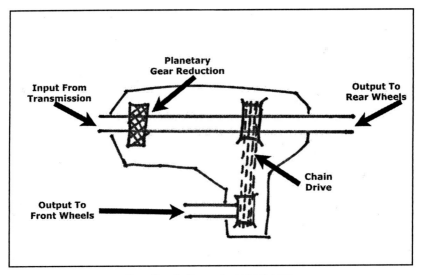

How a Transfer Case works, in simple terms

It turns out that this is a known problem with my car and several other models that use the same part. My car is a 2008, and it turns out in 2010, they redesigned the transfer case in such a way that, in theory, it would prevent the failure I was experiencing. I looked at all my options for fixing the car and they broke down as follows:

Option	Cost	Notes
New part installed by dealer	$Outrageous	Cleanest, but not an option due to cost
New part installed by independent mechanic	75% of $Outrageous	Still pretty clean, but still pretty expensive
New part installed by me	35% of $Outrageous	Now we're getting somewhere
Rebuilt part installed by me	23% of $Outrageous	Not enough info on how it was rebuilt and by whom, and it would still be the old design
Used part installed by me	15% of $Outrageous	Since all the used ones are the old design, this option is not fixing anything, only buying time
Rebuild kit applied to my failed part & installed by me	10% of $Outrageous	I'm good with cars, but this option was beyond my capabilities and comfort level

After more research and some online conversations with other folks who suffered the same failure, I opted for ordering a new, redesigned transfer case that would be installed by me.

The initial problem presented itself on a Sunday, and I drove the car for five days as I figured out what to do. On Friday afternoon I ordered the part from a place in Miami called Cobra Transmission. Paying $45 for UPS ground shipping, the part was scheduled to arrive the following Thursday.

Luckily the car was drivable. Since the all wheel drive system only sends power to the front wheels of my car when it needs to, I could keep the transfer case from making that awful noise by simply being gentle with the gas pedal.

RATHER QUICKLY THE PROBLEM GOT WORSE.

From the moment I ordered the new part, it seemed like the car knew I was going to rip it apart, and it was not pleased. By the end of the weekend, the problem was to the point where the only way to prevent the noise was to lift my foot off the brake and let the car accelerate using only the idle of the engine. Once I got up to 15 MPH, I could then give it a little gas and proceed as normal.

ON THE HIGHWAY, THE CAR WAS FINE, BUT AROUND TOWN I WAS REALLY PISSING PEOPLE OFF.

At intersections, the light would turn green and all I could do was release the brake and begin my slow roll up to speed. I was frequently on the receiving end of every form of angry driver "expression."

One afternoon I made a right turn out of our neighborhood onto a two-lane road with a speed limit of 35, this particular section of the road is marked with a double yellow line. A car that was at least 100 yards to my left when I pulled out, raced up to my bumper and recklessly crossed the double yellow to get around me. I was doing 30. A half mile later, I caught up to this individual as we both waited at a red light. I waved.

Whenever I had to wait to turn left across traffic, I made cautious choices that those behind me must have been frustrated to both watch and endure.

I even got the point where I would look far ahead at intersections and try to adjust my speed, so I would never have come to a stop. This made for some rather odd driving behavior, at least relative to the average American who likes to get to the red light as fast as possible.

Making matters worse, my car is of German extraction (even though it was built in Tuscaloosa Alabama) and because of this, people assume I will drive faster than average, not slower.

So there I was, for nearly a week, misbehaving in the eyes of every other motorist around me. I was moving slowly, unpredictably and in a way that was inconveniencing others. On the surface my car looked fine.

As someone pulled up behind me at a red light, they had no reason to believe that they were about to be infuriated by damaged part that they couldn't see.

As I kept landing in these situations, I found myself wanting to warn them, or at least explain that I was sorry for being such a pain in the ass, but there was simply no way to do so.

AFTER A COUPLE DAYS OF THIS I REALIZED SOMETHING...WHAT I WAS EXPERIENCING IS EXACTLY WHAT SOMEONE WITH A DISABILITY EXPERIENCES EVERY DAY.

Merriam Webster's Ninth Collegiate Dictionary defines disability as:

dis·abil·i·ty \ˌdis-ə-ˈbil-ət-ē\ *n* (1581) **1 a :** the condition of being disabled **b :** inability to pursue an occupation because of physical or mental impairment **2 :** lack of legal qualification to do something **3 :** a disqualification, restriction, or disadvantage

BY ANY INTERPRETATION, MY CAR AND I WERE DISABLED.

I was the person with MS, moving a little too slowly on the sidewalk or coming through the door at the mall. I was the person holding up the line at Starbucks, taking a little too long to place my order because of a brain injury. I was the person in the wheelchair getting in everyone's way.

By the time the man in the brown shorts delivered my package, the car was nearly un-drivable. On the final drive back to our garage I actually drove up the street with my hazards on. It turns out the closest thing to a blanket "I'm sorry" in the motoring world is the use of the 4-way flashers. Though to be honest, pushing that giant red triangle on the dashboard feels a lot more like "I'm pathetic" than "I'm sorry."

The old transfer case removed (back) and the shiny new one ready to install

The part arrived and it took me a few days to put it in, but when all was said and done, the repair worked. My car was restored to its non-clicking, all wheel driving, zippy self, and my driving has returned to normal.

I will admit that I am still a little gun-shy about the proverbial "pedal to the metal," since I do not ever want to hear that awful noise again. I can tell you though that I have a new appreciation for anyone I encounter who might not be acting "normal" as society defines it. None of us ever knows what is really going on in the mind, body or heart of another. We should at all times assume that everyone is doing their very best, and we should love them for the effort – no exceptions.

CAN YOU IMAGINE IF EVERYBODY DID THAT, EVEN FOR JUST ONE DAY?

So the next time a slow, old, Buick-driving, white-haired lady is making you late, think about where she might be going and the effort she is making just to get there. I'm betting your situation is a lot better than hers and "expressing yourself" really won't help either of you.

If the universe was trying to teach me a lesson by breaking my transfer case, as my anger and frustration spewed all over the temporarily closed streets of downtown Rochester that morning, then consider me an educated "transfer student." Well-played universe, well played.

This week's task is not just for a week. This one is forever. As you live your life stop trying to figure out how to get around the lady driving too slow in front of you, but instead try to imagine why she is going slow in the first place.

Every day you encounter people, things and circumstances in your way. From now on, make every effort to replace impatience with compassion.

I'm going to repeat that – every time something or someone gets your dander up, pause a moment to try and imagine what they are going through.

This will not be easy. In fact, it is counter to human nature, at least in society as we know it. But, if you are able to do it, you will begin to notice that your blood pressure will be lower, you'll be happier, and you will have a much greater appreciation for the world around you.

Here's the best part, you didn't have to spend five hours on your back fixing a car to get there.

48 – HOW OFTEN DO YOU CHANGE THE APPLES?

Dorothy Parker once famously said, "The cure for ignorance is curiosity. There is no cure for curiosity."

There might be people out there who would disagree with me, but I for one am very happy that there is no cure for curiosity, and I won't be contributing to anyone searching for such a cure – ever.

I give you three stories in the struggle to wipe ignorance from the face of the earth, once and for all.

ONE

One spring break while I was still in high school, my older brother came home from college for the week. At some point while he was home, his friend Adam came to visit for a few days.

To my sister and me, a college friend of our older brother's, was a new and different experience, but we really had no idea what to expect. Adam seemed like a nice enough guy, but he had this devilish look in his eye; the kind of look that made you want to hang out with him just to see what he might do. Although his name was Adam, everyone called him "Slick." After hearing my brother call him Slick a few times, I asked if I could call him Slick. I was told to call him Adam.

One afternoon during Adam's visit, we went to the local McDonalds. I can't say if it was for a meal or not, since at that time my brother and I would often swing through a McDonalds for a couple thousand calories whenever. Oh to have that metabolism once again.

So there we were, standing in line at the McDonalds at the corner of Rte. 250 and Penfield Rd. Adam was standing in front of my brother and me, and just as it was about to be his turn to order, he turned back to us and said, "watch this."

Adam proceeded to order a drink, a large fry and a Big Mac, but just as the unsuspecting clerk was about to give him his total, Adam piped up, "oh, about the Big Mac, can I have that with no meat?"

Stephen S. Nazarian

THE CLERK FROZE LIKE A COPY OF WINDOWS '95.

After a moment the clerk said, "um, did you just ask for your Big Mac without meat?" Adam politely replied, "yes I did. One Big Mac please, with no meat." The clerk grabbed the gooseneck microphone bolted to the counter and urgently called for a manager. The manager arrived and asked what the problem was. The clerk desperately replied, "this gentleman here is asking for a Big Mac with no meat, and I don't know what to do."

THEY BOTH STARED AT THE REGISTER THAT WAS COMPLETELY DEVOID OF A "NO MEAT" BUTTON.

The manager looked Adam straight in the eye and said, "sir, am I to understand that you are trying to order a Big Mac with no meat?" Without ever losing his completely straight face, Adam replied, "yes, that is what I ordered. Oh, and one more thing, since I'm not having any meat, can I have extra cheese?"

AT THIS POINT, BOTH THE CLERK'S AND THE MANAGER'S HEADS METAPHORICALLY EXPLODED.

In the end Adam got his vegetarian Big Mac, but it took about 10 minutes and several other McDonalds employees to figure out how to ring it up. He was not granted the requested extra cheese.

It turns out that Adam was not a vegetarian; he just wanted to see what would happen if he threw a fast-food curve ball at an unsuspecting minimum-wage worker. Of course I later found out that he also didn't care if I called him by his nickname, he just thought it would be fun to flatly deny me the permission to do so.

TWO

A few years after the now infamous "meatless mac incident," my college friend Stuart came to Cape Cod with my family and me. One morning we rose very early and went deep-sea fishing on a party boat called The Naviator, out of Welfleet harbor.

We had a fine time, caught many fish and enjoyed the banter between "Captain Jack" and his first mate, a wizened old man named Angelo. The trip came and went, but it was such a legendary day that we spoke of it often.

The following summer, Stuart didn't come to the cape, but my girlfriend Jill was with us. One afternoon we were having lunch in a pizzeria, and right there on the front of the pizza counter, was a poster advertising fishing trips on none other than "The Naviator."

228

Given how much fun we had on that trip the year before, I knew that Stuart would love that poster to hang on the wall of his dorm room. I was heading back to Lehigh a week later, so the timing was perfect. My sister and I sat there trying to figure out how we could "liberate" the poster without anyone noticing. We talked about a diversion, or waiting for the pizza guy to go into the back, but it was just talk.

As we discussed our options, Jill stood up, walked right up to the counter and said, "excuse me, do you see that guy over there, he's my boyfriend and he would really like this poster you have tacked to the front of your counter. It is just an advertisement for a fishing boat, but he wants it for his friend who once took a trip on that boat. He was going to steal it, but I figured better to ask, so would you mind if we took it?"

The infamous "Naviator" steaming along in the waters of Cape Cod Bay

THE PIZZA GUY WAS SO SURPRISED AT HER HONEST APPROACH THAT HE SAID, "UM, SURE, WHATEVER."

We finished our pizza and left with the poster. Stuart loved it.

THREE

One day in the fall of 2014 I was supposed to meet a friend for lunch at a restaurant here in Rochester. We managed to get our signals crossed on the meeting time, so I ended up having to wait for a while in the lobby of the restaurant as he hurriedly drove from his office to meet me.

When you enter this particular restaurant, you come in from the parking lot into an outer lobby. You then go through a second set of doors to an inner lobby to the hostess station.

AS I PACED BACK AND FORTH WAITING FOR MY FRIEND, I WENT IN AND OUT OF BOTH SETS OF DOORS SEVERAL TIMES.

On the walls of the outer lobby, they have these funky wooden shelves from the floor to the ceiling. On these shelves, the restaurant has placed hundreds of green apples. It is actually pretty cool because that many apples in such a small space creates an unavoidable wave of apple smell. It is as pleasant as it is unusual.

The "wall of apples" at the Next Door Bar & Grill

I walked by the apples a few times not thinking much about them, but as I sat on the bench next to the hostess' podium, I began to think about the apples.

- How many apples are there?

- What variety are they?

- Is the smell from the apples alone or do they spray the outer lobby with some kind of "apple cologne" to get the smell-o-vision effect to work?

- How often do they change the apples?

As I pondered these mysteries, I received a text from my friend saying that he was seven minutes away. Up to now, the hostess had been very friendly, but I was beginning to see that she thought my lunch friend might be imaginary. So, I walked right up to her and asked:

"HOW OFTEN DO YOU CHANGE THE APPLES?"

She did not seem at all surprised by the question and she definitely knew the answer, and then some.

She told me that they change them every few weeks, and as they ripen the smell gets stronger. Some varieties last longer than others.

These particular apples happened to be granny smiths, and since we'd had a relatively cool summer, the apples had been lasting longer than usual. They do go check the apples every day and swap out any individual apples that have gone bad. People ask all the time if they ever use other fruit, but they only use apples. Apparently, I was the first to ever ask about the changing frequency.

How often are you curious about something, but you stop shy of asking the question that would turn your curiosity to knowledge?

Adam wanted to see what would happen – he found out.

Jill wanted Stuart to have the poster – she got it.

I was curious about the apples – now I know.

Most people really are nice, and want to talk about their lives, their jobs and their situations. All you have to do is ask. If everyone did more of this, ignorance wouldn't stand a chance; and wouldn't that be a wonderful thing.

Here is this week's challenge. Go out and ask one question every day for the next seven days. Ask about something stupid, something fun, something that before today you wouldn't have bothered about. When someone you know expresses curiosity about something, stand right up and get the answer for them.

They say that the only dumb questions are the ones you don't ask. Well, what are you waiting for?

Stephen S. Nazarian

49 – I DON'T THINK HE REALLY HAS A GUN

In 1992, I lived in New York City. My apartment was at 435 East 74th St, between 1st and York Avenues. It was a five story walk-up and I lived on the first floor in something they called a ½ bedroom apartment.

How can you have ½ of a bedroom you ask? Well there was a separate room for sleeping, but it was so small that it had no door, and the queen-sized futon mattress I had shoved into one corner, had to have the opposite corner curled up to make room for a small dresser. I guess it's a ½ bedroom when the room doesn't have enough space for the whole bed.

The door to my apartment building

I moved into the apartment in January, and some time that spring, my parents came to New York to attend a medical meeting. They were staying at the New York Hilton on 6th Avenue. One morning my Dad was busy with meetings so my Mom decided to walk from their hotel to my apartment. Once she arrived, we planned to take the bus the length of Manhattan to Battery Park, where we would take a ferry out to the newly renovated Ellis Island.

My Mom arrived on time, but seemed a little flustered. As she sat down in my tiny living room, I got her a glass of water. After a minute or two she looked up at me and said, "Yesterday I had to pay $12 for a chicken sandwich and a Snapple, and this morning as I walked here I don't think I heard one person speak English."

I looked back at her saying, "Mom, that's New York." She shook her head and said, "Well okay then, we better get going." I was thinking I might be in for a pretty long day.

We had a nice ride on the M-15 bus, taking about an hour to cover the seven miles of our journey. It was by no means fast, but when you take the subway in New York, you see the subway tunnels.

WHEN YOU TAKE THE BUS, YOU SEE NEW YORK.

We got off the bus and had a few blocks to cover to get to the ferry. As we rounded a corner, near the famous Wall Street Bull, my Mom saw a homeless woman sleeping along the side of a building, partly covered in a blanket of corrugated cardboard. She looked up at me and said, "Stephen, we need to help that woman."

MY MOTHER IS A NURSE AND IN GENERAL A VERY NICE PERSON, BUT THIS REQUEST WAS NOT GOING TO BE GRANTED.

I looked at my 5' 8" fair-skinned Swedish Mother, who was wearing a turtleneck and a gold cross on a gold chain and said, "Mom, how do you know if that woman needs or wants help? Furthermore, if you kneel down to 'help' her she could easily rip the your cross and gold chain right off your neck, and take off down the street with your purse. So, as much as I'd like to assist you in helping that woman, we are going to walk right by her and into the park."

CLEARLY SHOCKED BY WHAT I SAID (ON SEVERAL LEVELS) SHE LOOKED BACK AT ME AND SAID, "STEPHEN, NEW YORK HAS MADE YOU HARD!"

In that moment, she was probably a bit disappointed in me, but the education I was getting in New York was multi-faceted, but it wouldn't be long before my new instincts would pay dividends; only about eight hours actually.

Mom and I had a fine time at Ellis Island, and on our way back to the hotel, we took the subway. I dropped her off around 4:00 with the plan being for me to meet them back in the hotel lobby at 7:00 for dinner.

After moving to Manhattan, I discovered two things very quickly:

1. You should never buy more groceries than you can reasonably carry yourself

2. Checking accounts in the city are outrageously expensive unless you have a crap-ton of money in the bank

It was this second fact of life in Manhattan that plays into the story. I got paid every week, but since I couldn't afford a bank account, I would go to the issuing bank of my payroll check and cash it there. I would then use cash for most things, and buy money orders for the rest.

THE DOWNSIDE TO THIS PLAN WAS THAT AT TIMES, I HAD AS MUCH AS $1,000 CASH ON HAND IN ONE FORM OR ANOTHER.

I met my parents at the appointed time and we headed out to the subway, which was the BDFM (orange) line. We hopped on a B or D train heading downtown. We were going to a restaurant on 18th street, so we would to take the train to 16th and walk the two blocks back uptown.

The train got us to our stop in short order, and we disembarked. Instead of going right up to street level, I saw that the tunnels could take us to all the way to an exit on 18th, and since it was raining it made sense to go that way. We took one flight of stairs up to the concourse level between the tracks and the street, and made our way, with some other random folks, underground towards the 18th street exit.

We were about fifty yards from the final staircase up to the sidewalk when a man popped out of a doorway, and while pointing something at us through his jacket pocket said, "I have a gun, give me all your money, and jewelry!" Of course this was not good, in many ways; not the least of which was the fact that I had $900 in cash in my wallet that I was planning to use to pay my rent the next day.

Without missing a step, I grabbed my parents by the elbows and kept them moving. We walked right by the "man with the gun" and as we approached the stairs to safety, I confidently stated, "I don't think he really has a gun." My confidence was contagious because other folks nearby also ignored the man's declaration, following me, Mom and Dad.

We passed through the archway, and as we began to climb it looked like we were home free – until we turned the corner on the switchback stairs and saw the locked gate.

OH SHIT, WE'RE ALL GOING TO DIE.

We all stood there silently for a moment, and then we did the only thing we could do, we went back down the stairs and find another way out. I exchanged glances with some of the others and, it was easy to see who among us were New Yorkers.

We got to the bottom of the stairs and turned towards where the man had been, but he was gone. We covered the seventy-five or so yards to another exit, and made it up to the street.

When the three of us got to the restaurant, the hostess showed us to our table and before she turned to leave, my mother ordered a gin and tonic without being asked. Now, my Mom is not a complete teetotaler, but I had never (nor have I since) seen her lead the charge to the bar.

Our drinks arrived and my Dad, said "c'mon Steve, admit you were a little scared back there." I admitted about 10% of what I was feeling, because I think any more might have killed them, right there at the table. We enjoyed our dinner and as we rose from the table, my Dad insisted on springing for a cab. I didn't argue.

There is another chapter in this book called *The Power Of The Clipboard*; the point of which was simple: look like you know what you're doing and people will leave you alone.

That day in New York was all about knowing my surroundings and how to behave within them. I made an educated bet that a guy with an actual gun would be going after bigger fish than a handful of subway riders. A "finger gun in a jacket pocket," was much more likely.

Was I scared? You bet I was, and if my parents hadn't been there I might have lost $900 in cash, but my brain kicked into full-on "protection mode," and it paid off. We humans make some of our best, and boldest moves when we have the most to lose. It is when things are less intense we tend to be more careful.

I challenge you this week to take a low-risk and careful situation and kick it up a notch. Go with your gut and make a bold move.

Chances are whomever you're facing doesn't really have a gun in his pocket; but much like that night in New York, if you win the contest of confidence you'll never really know, and in the end it won't actually matter.

---

50 – TWO OUT OF THREE

Back in March 1994, I had a one-day job in New York City. The job didn't pay very much; in fact, it didn't pay anything.

Okay I may be generalizing a bit. I had a one-day gig volunteering at the **36th Annual Grammy Awards** at Radio City Music Hall.

That experience itself warrants an entire chapter of its own, but on that chilly Saturday on Sixth Avenue, I spent the better part of five hours with one of the icons of my youth. He was born Michael Lee Aday, but you all probably know him better by his stage name: Meat Loaf.

On July 31, 1977, Meat Loaf (or Mr. Loaf as I heard many people call him) released *Two Out of Three Ain't Bad*. It topped-out at #11 on the Billboard Hot 100, but I bet nearly everyone reading his (save my children) can sing the song.

The chorus goes like this:

I want you, oh, I need you
But there ain't no way I'm ever gonna love you
Now don't be sad, oh, 'cause two out of three ain't bad
Now don't be sad no 'cause two out of three ain't bad

As bittersweet as the sentiment is, I have found, in the thirty-seven plus years since I heard it first, that two out of three equals 66.66% and although technically a passing grade, it often leads to pretty solid failure.

My college friend Stuart had a bit of an interesting set-up in his house in high school. At some point in he early teen years, his parents built an addition on their house so his father's parents could come live with them.

HIS GRANDMOTHER WAS SUFFERING FROM ALZHEIMER'S, AND BY MOVING IN WITH HIS FAMILY THEY COULD ALL HELP WITH HER CARE.

They lived like this for several years and as it always the case his grandmother finally succumbed to the disease. Stu's grandfather, Alan, had dedicated so much of his time to the care of his wife that after she died, he found himself with way too much free time on his hands.

RATHER THAN LOOK BACK TO THINGS HE USED TO DO, HE DECIDED TO VENTURE FORWARD AND TRY SOME NEW ACTIVITIES.

Living in suburban Pennsylvania, he had access to fresh produce both in the family garden behind the house and at local farms. One morning he decided today was the day he would make zucchini bread.

He found a recipe and gathered up the ingredients. By the time he was in full swing with his project, all of the other members of Stu's family had gone to work or school. Alan was alone in the house. The zucchini was from a local farm, and as the recipe instructed, he shredded the long green squash with the coarse side of a box grater.

When the shredding was done, he measured what he had. The recipe called for four cups of shredded zucchini, he only had three.

Looking at the other details, Alan decided that finding more zucchini was going to be easier than trying to reduce the other measurements by ¼. So, out into the garden he went.

After stretching his tall frame to the ground to examine what was available on the collection of plants, he found what he figured was a suitable solution to his problem. He returned to the kitchen, finished his shredding, executed the rest of the recipe and popped the two loaf pans into the oven.

WHEN STU AND HIS FAMILY RETURNED FROM THEIR BUSY DAYS, ALAN PRESENTED THEM WITH THE RESULTS OF HIS EFFORTS.

The loaves looked mostly okay, but where normal zucchini bread is as tall is as it is wide, what Alan had prepared looked, well, short. They cut the bread, slathered it with butter and dug in. It smelled and tasted like zucchini bread, but it was bit like biting into a gooey brick. It was perhaps the densest sweet bread ever served in Chester County Pennsylvania.

So close, yet still so far away

When Stu's grandfather had ventured into the garden, he had not found any zucchini. All he could find was a cucumber.

- ✓ Green like a zucchini – check.
- ✓ Long and cylindrical like a zucchini – check.
- ✗ Same density and moisture content as a zucchini – yeah, no

The fall of 2014 was the 50th running of the McQuaid Cross-Country Invitational. The meet that year saw nearly 8,000 runners from high schools allover the northeast. Our two oldest boys Lewis and Oliver both run cross-country for McQuaid Jesuit.

A race gets underway at the McQuaid Invitational

One of the things the school does for this event is arrange housing for some of the visiting teams. They used to coordinate housing for any school attending the meet, and in fact we hosted teams when I ran cross-country in high school.

As the meet has grown over the years, the coordination effort simply got too large, so now McQuaid limits the housing offer to other Jesuit high schools. This year we were fortunate to house four lovely young ladies from Walsh Jesuit in Cuyahoga Falls, OH.

The school holds a spaghetti dinner where the visitors and host families meet up. Since we had three of our kids along, plus the four girls to transport home, my wife and I had to bring two cars to the school. When dinner was complete, Emily took Lewis and Lawrence home and I followed about twenty minutes later with Oliver and the four girls.

OLIVER DOES WELL WITH THE LADIES.

When we got home, we unloaded all of the many suitcases, sleeping bags and pillows. We set the girls up in the finished basement where there are two couches and a giant beanbag chair. Given the lanky size of the girls, I offered to go get our double-sized Areobed to give them additional sleeping options. They sized up the room and said, "Yes please."

I came upstairs and told Emily that we needed the Aerobed. She replied, "I already plugged the pump in to charge, so in 30 minutes we can pump it up."

I did a few things around the house, and as I walked by the place in the hall closet where we charge all of our devices, out of the corner of my eye I saw the Areobed pump plugged in for charging. Twenty minutes later I plunked myself into the chair next to Emily who was using her iPad on the couch.

"The Wi-Fi isn't working" Emily proclaimed as I put my feet up on the ottoman. This is not an uncommon statement in our house, though the problem is most often, um; well let's call it "user misunderstanding."

Without leaving the comfort of my perch, I pulled my phone out to check the Wi-Fi, fully expecting to find nothing wrong with it. To my surprise it was

A reenactment of what I saw in the hall closet that evening

actually down. I would not find any traces of "Nazarian 143," the access point that I had just given to the girls downstairs. "Well that's embarrassing," I thought to myself as I got up to investigate the problem.

As I walked away from the couch, I turned to Emily and asked, "did you unplug the access point to charge the Areobed pump?" Without looking up from her iPad game of Scrabble she replied, "I don't know what an access point is, but I borrowed a wire from one of your blinking boxes in the closet."

Sure enough she had unplugged the Wi-Fi access point, but it was worse than that. Instead of unplugging the Wi-Fi power adapter from the power strip and using the adapter that came with the pump, she had simply pulled the wire out of the Wi-Fi blinking box and plugged it into the pump.

- ✓ It plugs into the wall and provides electricity – check
- ✓ The plug from the "blinking box" fits into the pump – check
- ✗ Is the voltage the same? – What exactly do you mean by "voltage?"

The adapter for the Wi-Fi is 12 volts DC. The Aerobed pump requires 9 volts DC.

I PUMPED UP THE AEROBED USING MY SHOP VAC.

As we review things in our lives, on the surface many things look the same. Even after digging a little deeper, they may still look like a match, but sometimes close enough just isn't close enough.

In Meat Loaf's world two out of three may not be too bad, but for my experience I can tell you that most of the time it sure ain't good.

Your job this week is to zero in on the accuracy of the matches in your life.

Sure, sometimes good enough is good enough, and I have always been a fan of the axiom "never let perfection get in the way of the good." However, the good you seek must be sufficient to get the job done right, not just grand you the ability to say, "I did the job."

Nobody wants to spend the night on a flat Aerobed with a belly full of gooey zucchini bread – nobody.

Stephen S. Nazarian

51 – SEVERE TIRE DAMAGE

In *A Servant To Servants*, Robert Frost opines,

> **He says the best way out is always through.**
> **And I can agree to that, or in so far**
> **As that I can see no way out but through.**

Ever since the development of the "undo" command on personal computers, we as a people have become reliant on the idea that something done wrong can be reversed. As much as an immediate "undo" of a keystroke or click can be both convenient and without consequence, trying to revert from an undesirable state to a previous one is sometimes (as Frost suggests) perhaps not the best path to take.

===

Some time while she was in college, my sister and her friends took a spring break trip to somewhere warm. On this trip they flew to their destination, and rented a car at the airport.

FROM WHAT I RECALL, THEY DROVE THE RENTAL CAR AROUND FOR THE WEEK WITHOUT INCIDENT.

When it was time to head back to the airport, they did not leave sufficient time to find their way, return the car, and get to their flight without a mad dash. So, with no time to spare, they entered the labyrinth that is the rental car return area, OF EVERY AIRPORT IN AMERICA.

Given that they were a pack of college girls trying to savor the last morsels of their spring break, I'm guessing that the cooperative communication in the car was not functioning as well as it could have.

As the driver drove, the passengers hastily read signs and pointed in the directions that each thought the driver should go.

THERE WAS LITTLE, IF ANY CONSENSUS.

After several laps around the driveways and ramps, the driver made a command decision and drove into one of the return lanes. As they crossed over the one-way barrier embedded in the road, the large signs before them made it abundantly clear that they were in the wrong place.

Without hesitation, the driver shifted the car into reverse, and raised her right arm over the passenger seat, while turning her head to look out the back window.

IF YOU'VE DONE SOMETHING WRONG, YOU SHOULD IMMEDIATELY TRY AND UNDO IT, RIGHT?

Well, as the driver began to move in reverse, my sister screamed STOP! As mentioned above, the girls had driven over one of those one-way barriers that if you drive over the wrong way will result in "Severe Tire Damage."

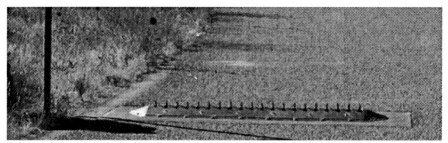

The one-way barrier my sister's friends thought they could back over

This warning has always struck me as odd since the result of such a move will always be complete tire destruction. As foreboding as "severe tire damage" may sound, it does imply that whatever is about to happen could possibly be fixed. This is simply not true.

Fortunately, for the girls, my sister's siren cry prevented them from adding, "rental car tire shredding" to their list of delays. They were able to find their way out, and return the car to the proper destination. I have no idea if they made their scheduled flight; I only remember the story you've just read.

From 1969 to 1973, we lived on a cute little circular street in Penfield, NY called "Pleasant Way." It wasn't all circle, in fact you came onto the street on a little leg, which at a small intersection, turned into a circle. You can see what I mean from the satellite on the next page.

Some time in the late spring of 1972, my mother was driving her 1971 Ford Ranch Wagon home in the mid-afternoon. The Ranch Wagon was Ford's, full size station wagon at the time and not only was it HUGE, it weighed in at more than two tons.

As we pulled into the neighborhood, we were stuck behind a school bus dropping of the local children. This was an elementary bus, and since there were kindergarteners aboard, the bus was stopping frequently.

Pleasant Way as it appears today via Google Earth

Because of the circular, no-through-traffic, nature of the street, activity in the neighborhood was very laid back. Kids and dogs played in the street all the time, since the only people who ever drove down the street were our neighbors, the mailman and school buses. Among the neighborhood residents was a large mutt of a dog named Queenie.

QUEENIE WAS A MELLOW DOG, SO MELLOW IN FACT THAT SHE WOULD REGULARLY SLEEP RIGHT IN THE MIDDLE OF THE ROAD, ESPECIALLY ON WARM SUNNY DAYS.

When the bus snuffed its red flashing lights and moved on, my mom let her foot off the brake and began to move forward. Just a moment after we began to roll, the left side of the car rose and fell twice, as if we'd run over something in the road. My mother immediately stopped the car and put it in reverse, backing up to see what was going on.

It turns out, as we had waited behind the big yellow school bus, Queenie had ambled over and took her place in the street; right between the back of the bus and the front of the Nazarian Ranch Wagon.

My mother had driven her 4,100 pound car over Queenie with both left wheels, only to put the car in reverse – and do it AGAIN.

By some miracle Queenie was unhurt by all this, and after a trip to the vet was declared okay. The tread marks from the Ford did remain in her furry coat for several days, but eventually even those faded.

WINSTON CHURCHILL ONCE SAID, "IF YOU'RE GOING THROUGH HELL, KEEP GOING."

I think both Churchill and Frost were on to something. Unlike the quick undo in a piece of software, our lives are usually not best served by trying to get back what has been lost or damaged. Instead of trying to go back, we should keep going, and using what we've learned, figure the way out by going through.

It is normal to yearn for "the good old days" (even if it was only yesterday) but all we really have any control of is today and tomorrow. If we focus on where we're going instead of where we've been, we will daily do better and avoid any severe tire damage along the way.

This week you may not spend any time or effort worrying about what has happened. When troubles present themselves, you may acknowledge what has transpired, but you may not put forth any more energy than that.

All of your efforts, thoughts, sweat and momentum must be expended in a forward-looking direction.

Since the only two things you have any control over are today and tomorrow, that is where your focus should be. Since you can't change the past, give a polite nod to its existence and move on. If you give it more power than it deserves, it will own you, and that is far worse than shredded tires run over a lazy dog, I promise.

---

52 – CHRISTMAS EVE BUSINESS CARD

In December 1995 my life was good. Just the month before I had closed on my very first house. I truly loved my job in the professional audio electronics business; I had a nice group of friends, a church where I felt comfortable, and two great dogs. I didn't have a girlfriend, but with all the other stuff going so well, I figured that part of my life would come together soon enough. I was twenty-seven.

As most single, twenty-something guys do, I traveled back home to my parent's for Christmas. I don't remember exactly when I came home, but it was probably the day of the 23rd, just in time for my mom's annual Christmas party.

By this time in my life, Nazarian Christmas Eve was run on a consistent schedule. Around 5:30, we would sit-down to a dinner, made up of mostly Swedish dishes.

FOR THOSE WHO THINK THE SWEDES EAT ONLY WHAT YOU'VE SEEN IN AN IKEA CAFETERIA, AND DRINK ABSOLUT VODKA, LET ME TELL YOU NOW... THEY CHOW DOWN ON SOME CRAZY STUFF AT CHRISTMAS TIME.

From the rye bread dipped in pork broth, to the creamed codfish, and the (my personal favorite) jellied veal. Yes, you read that right; they mix up cooked, ground veal with clear, flavorless Jell-o, mold it into a brick, slice it like meatloaf and soak it in vinegar. It must be true since no sane person would make that up.

For dessert we would have rice pudding. Hidden in one of the cups of rice pudding was an almond. If you got the almond in yours, you were declared "king for the day." All that really meant was that you didn't have to do any dishes.

We ate early so my parents could get to church in time to sing in the choir at the early service. They would stay at church between services and then around 10:30, the rest of us would pile into cars and head downtown for the 11:00, candlelight service.

The church we grew up attending is actually in the city of Rochester NY, even though we lived ten miles away in a suburb, so attending

Christmas Eve service usually turned into a de facto reunion with all the church friends you didn't encounter elsewhere.

Billy is five or six years my junior, so I knew him, and we were friends, but not good friends. We had always shared a common interest in live music. After a quick handshake, the conversation went something like this:

Billy: So how's it going man?

Steve: Pretty good, how about you?

Billy: Awesome! What are you up to?

Steve: Well, I just bought my first house, I have a great job at an audio electronics company, and my buddy and me just launched in independent record label.

Billy: So, cool. You see any shows?

Steve: Actually, yeah. I go to a lot of concerts as part of my job and I've been doing live mixing for another buddy's band, so I get into New York City all the time.

Billy: Sounds like the scene is really going-off in New York.

Steve: I guess you could say that, I mean it is New York after all. So, Billy, what are you up to?

Billy: I'm down in Florida.

Steve: Oh cool, what are you doing?

Billy: Right now I'm selling daiquiris on the beach in Panama City, but I'm looking at some other stuff. Man, I'd love to come check out all that shit going on in New York.

Steve: Here's my business card. If you ever get up that way, give me a call.

Billy: Dude, I so will.

And so it was. Billy and I went our separate ways into the candle-filled church to celebrate the arrival of the baby Jesus. That should have been the end of the story but alas, we're just getting started.

I enjoyed Christmas with my family and a couple days later, my two dogs and I returned to our newly acquired "handyman special" in Greenwood Lake NY, a scant 3 miles from the New Jersey border.

I went back to work. A week later I enjoyed a fine New Year's Eve with friends in NYC, where we saw They Might Be Giants at a midnight show, in a tiny club.

All-in-all 1996 was looking pretty good. A few weeks later I was sitting at my desk when my phone rang:

Steve: Marketing, Steve speaking.

Voice: Dude, were you serious?

Steve: I'm not sure. Who is this?

Voice: Dude! It's Billy.

Steve: Billy who?

Well, it turns out that when Billy went to fly home to Florida after Christmas, his flight was overbooked. The airline offered a free round-trip to anyone willing to wait until the next available flight. Billy enthusiastically accepted.

He was calling to see if it was still okay for him to come "check out the scene" in New York. I said that it was, and we generally discussed the idea of him coming for a visit but didn't talk specifics.

A few weeks later I got another call with a date and a time he would be arriving. He was going to get a ride to my house from a friend. He didn't say how long he was planning to stay, and foolishly I neglected to ask.

Billy arrived. He had more stuff with him than I expected, and after a few hours of conversation it was clear that he had left Florida for good and this "visit" with me was going to be the platform from which he planned to launch "Billy 2.0."

I HAD ONLY MYSELF TO BLAME FOR THIS MISUNDERSTANDING, THAT WAS NOW GOING TO BE LIVING IN MY HOUSE FOR WHO KNEW HOW LONG.

Before I go on, let me paint you a picture. My new house had functionally one bedroom. The room that was once a kitchen was being transformed into a laundry/mud room, complete with a "dog den" for my two canines. The room that was once the second bedroom was partially torn apart as it was going to become the kitchen. The bathroom was functional, but far from complete.

The largest room in the house was the living room, one wall of which was a makeshift kitchen comprised of a fridge, a two-burner camp stove, a microwave and a coffeemaker; all placed atop a section of counter resting on two cheap filing cabinets. At the other end of the living room was a giant fireplace next to which I had placed my TV and stereo.

The TV got no over-the-air reception, and I was in no position to be paying for cable, so for the first eighteen months I lived in this house the only TV was rented VHS tapes.

So, there was Billy, sleeping on an air mattress in my deconstructed extra bedroom, eating my food, drinking my beer and with little else to do, that's pretty much all he did. Don't get me wrong, he was energetic and really wanted to launch some new kind of life, but his plan to do so consisted only what I've told you so far – nothing else.

A few days in, I took him to my office for the day. I gave him the comprehensive tour of the whole factory, and introduced him to some people who might be interested in hiring such a young man. The company wasn't hiring in any of the areas where he was even a tad qualified, but they took his resume (such as it was) and said they'd keep him in mind.

I had my little Saturn SL1 that I drove to work, but I also had a 1976, full size Chevrolet Suburban that I used as a sort of "rolling dumpster" for the work I was doing on the house. I told Billy he could use the Suburban to drive into town if he needed anything.

Every day I would head off to work with Billy asleep in "his" room. I would return at the end of the day and make dinner for us both. While I had been gone, Billy didn't do much other than drive the Suburban into town to buy beer and rent movies. After dinner he would help me with work on the house, but by 11:00 I would be ready for bed and Billy would inevitably settle in with another movie and a six-pack.

HE HAD A FEW HUNDRED BUCKS WITH HIM WHEN HE ARRIVED, BUT BEER AND VIDEO RENTALS GOBBLED IT UP PRETTY FAST.

After weeks of this routine, I realized that I was going to have to be the catalyst to help Billy get his act together. The next day I walked around to the people in my company who could hire him and they all gave me a polite but firm "not gonna happen."

I CAME HOME THAT NIGHT WITH "PLAN B."

Billy had decent experience working with bands, and knew a lot about live sound. Better yet, the only qualifications for getting into that kind of work are experience and connections. Billy had experience and I had the connections.

250

BILLY DIDN'T KNOW IT YET, BUT HE WAS GOING ON TOUR.

With whom I didn't really care, but it solved two problems at once; it got Billy and job and it got him the hell out of my house. By the time we got his resume cleaned up, and sent it in to the top twenty-five tour sound companies in the country, he had been living with me for more than a month.

To help his chances of landing even the lowest touring job out there, I pulled every industry string I had. We sent the packages out and waited, deciding that two weeks was the right amount of time to wait before following up by phone.

The following weekend I drove up to Massachusetts to visit some friends. I left after work on Friday leaving Billy alone in the house with the two dogs. When I returned Sunday afternoon, it was clear that Billy had not been alone. When I pressed him a little he admitted that an old girlfriend had come late Friday night and had stayed through noon Sunday. I told him that had he asked I certainly would have said it was okay, but that I didn't appreciate the sneaky nature of his actions. He apologized, but then looking at me said, "what else is wrong, I can see it in your face."

I exhaled saying simply, "Well, you managed to have a girl over in my new house, something I haven't been able to pull that off yet." He looked genuinely sorry and said, "Was that wrong?" I replied, "Only because you didn't ask."

It was at this moment I realized that I had stumbled into the worst possible set of circumstances. I functionally had a child living under my roof with me, for whom I was responsible, however because he was legally an adult (and not actually my child), I had no parental power whatsoever. Ugh.

The next week and a half went by quick enough with Billy's sleep-movie-dinner-movie-beer routine continuing with alarming consistency. He had helped me a good bit with work on the house, finishing the assembly and staining of the new cabinets for the laundry room. Hanging them was definitely going to be easier with two sets of hands.

By my calendar he should start making follow-up calls on Wednesday morning. As I drove home Tuesday evening, I practiced my pep-talk to get him ready for success.

THIS HAD TO WORK – I HAD NO "PLAN C."

As I pulled into the driveway, something wasn't right. Some lights were on in the house, but the Suburban was gone. I had a very bad feeling.

I walked into the house to find Billy sitting in the dark at the kitchen table with a hoodie pulled over his head. He looked up at me and said nothing. I sat down and asked where the Suburban might be and he told me the following:

He had awoken Tuesday morning, and figuring it had almost been two weeks he was going to call all the tour sound companies to follow up on his applications. He thought that just maybe he might get some good news so that when I got home we could celebrate. Unfortunately, that plan was not to be.

One by one, Billy had called all the companies, and one by one they told him to take a hike. You see, 1995 had been the biggest summer in the history of the tour sound business, and even though 1996 was shaping up nicely, the industry was shrinking, making no room for a newbie like Billy.

After being rejected twenty-five times in a row, Billy thought he best do something positive, so he decided to put the doors back on the cabinets we had just finished staining. As he began, he did not notice that there were two different lengths of screw, and rather quickly he managed to use a long one where he should have used a short one, driving the screw right through the front of a brand new cabinet door.

Looking at the undesired hole he had just made in the once pristine door, he panicked and decided he had to go to town, get some wood putty and clean up the mess he had just made. Billy had a problem though; he had no money, at least not normal money. He did however have a coffee can full of change.

HE HOPPED INTO THE SUBURBAN, FOLGERS CAN IN HAND AND HEADED INTO TOWN.

The Suburban was a little rough. It would start cold, but once it was warmed up it didn't like to start again until it had cooled off. This didn't bother me since I never shut if off at the dump, and I was normally in Home Depot long enough for it to cool down. It also had a tendency to smoke a bit at idle, well maybe more than a bit.

For some reason Billy thought the hardware store wouldn't take $2.75 in change in exchange for a jar of wood putty, so first he went to the bank. Since he didn't want to get stuck in the bank parking lot with a car that wouldn't start, so he put it in park and left it running while he went in to exchange his can-o-coins for paper money.

As he stood in line Billy was hoping his luck was about to change. He would get the money, get the wood putty, fix the door and have the cabinets all put together before I got home. It was then he heard the sirens.

The idling Suburban had begun to smoke so badly that someone called the fire department. When Billy emerged from the bank, they were hosing down the car and a policeman was inquiring about the owner. Billy stepped up, but he had another problem. The entire time I had been letting him drive my cars he actually had a suspended license.

THEY IMPOUNDED MY SUBURBAN AND PUT BILLY IN THE BACK OF THE POLICE CAR.

He wasn't actually arrested, but he did receive a violation of some kind for the smoking car, in addition to being cited for driving on a suspended license. The local cop felt sorry for him and gave him a ride home.

By the time I got home, Billy had been on the phone with a recruiter from the Army, but I guess they weren't impressed with his recent activity and told him to call back after he "got his act together." Holy shit, what a mess.

I got the Suburban out of impound, but told Billy in no uncertain terms that he had to get a job and fast.

Within a few days he found a listing for a job at an audio rental company in Manhattan that I had actually used at one point. He put in an application, and as a former customer I called in the next day and put in good word. Within the week he had the job, but my long road was far from over.

After taxes and bus fare in and out of the city, his check didn't leave nearly enough for rent of any kind. So, for the next few months he went to work every day (an improvement) but he was still living in my house and I would often have to go get him from the bus at 11pm or later.

One Saturday he went into the city to go "clubbing" with some friends, and he said he would be late so he would get a cab from the bus back to the house. At 4:00am my phone rang. When I answered, it was a collect call from Billy.

He had finished his night out and was napping at the Port Authority Bus Terminal waiting for the first morning bus. As he slept someone robbed him of all his cash. He was broke and stuck in the city.

UP I GOT, AND INTO THE CITY I DROVE.

Little by little, Billy started to show some responsibility, and the folks he was working for even offered to pay for him to take a course so he could get his license back. They needed a delivery driver and they liked Billy. Better yet, the driver position was much better pay.

It took another two months, but Billy finally found an apartment he could afford and moved out. He had been in my house the better part of five months.

I never added it all up, but I guess by the time he left, Billy's little "residence" had cost me close to $1,000, and that was in actual cash outlay; not including food, utilities and other intangibles.

Until he was actually gone I didn't even realize how much stress his presence had placed upon me. I was mentally and physically exhausted. I cleaned my house from top to bottom and swore to myself that if I ever had another roommate of any kind her name had to be Mrs. Nazarian, no exceptions.

I heard from Billy a few times after he moved out, but then I lost track of him. In 1999 I did get a new roommate, and her name wasn't Mrs. Nazarian; no, it was Dr. Nazarian and despite my earlier statement of no exceptions, it was a minor deviation I was willing to accept.

Not long after we got married I sold my first house, leaving Greenwood Lake and that chapter of my life solidly in the past. Dr. Nazarian and I started our life together in a cute Cape Cod in Penfield NY. In June 2000, I got another roommate in the form of our first child Charlotte. She was no help around the house at all, but she didn't drink beer and as far as I knew her license had never been suspended.

One day in early 2001 I came home from work and in the mail was a card addressed to me. It wasn't Christmas nor my birthday and I didn't recognize the return address. I was intrigued as I opened the envelope, half expecting to find some kind of clever sales pitch disguised as a card.

The card had a festive "Thank You" emblazoned on the front and what I found inside stopped me dead in my tracks. I have since misplaced the card so I will have to paraphrase what it said (at least how I remember it). The handwritten note went something like this:

Dear Steve,

I know it has been a while since you heard from me, but I wanted to update you on how I've been doing. After moving into the city, I worked for that company for a while, but through that job I met some guys who own a recording studio in New Jersey.

I now have a great job working in that studio, I am married and we have a baby girl.

I don't know if I was ever able to tell you how much your support meant to me those years ago when you took me into your home. I was lost, I had no direction and you stood by my side while I figured it out. I'm not sure how you did it, and I'm not sure why you did, but I can say for sure that I sure am glad you did.

You saved my life and I don't know if I can ever thank you enough.

Best to you and your family.

Billy

I was speechless. From the day he moved out I had always assumed that he had landed at my door as some kind of lesson, some kind of test, some kind of thing the universe was trying to teach me, and perhaps all of that is still true. What I didn't realize was that for every thing I thought Billy was taking from me, I was in fact giving him something.

Maybe he didn't realize it at the time, but when he put it all together, everything I did for him actually added up to something. Something worth way more than the grand it cost me.

We all have periods in our lives that seem unnecessarily burdened and devoid of meaning. My friend Bob Goff would tell you that when in doubt, just love, and you will never regret it.

The day Billy showed up, neither one of us knew why he was there. The day he left we were both glad he'd moved on. The day that card came I finally understood what it all meant.

This story was last for a reason. When you started reading this book, you expected that the stories and ideas would show you how to improve your life, and I hope this has been the case. The thing that was less clear from the subtitle of "How everything you do is like money in the bank," is this:

The "money" you earn from the things that you do, is not always deposited in to your account, at least not immediately.

This week's challenge is a combination of all the challenges that have come before. Take all the ideas, lessons, notions and concepts, and open them up to the world beyond yourself.

An investment in someone else is an investment in yourself, and the return on that is much larger than a Folgers can full of change.

CONCLUSION

Thank you for taking a year of your life to share some of my adventures with me. Much like two people seeing different things in a great work of art, I hope that you have taken something personal and meaningful from the words on these pages, something beyond just words on the page.

My hope is that you will take your experience as a launching pad from which you will live a richer and more meaningful life. I wrote the book; the rest is up to you.

I will leave you with one last challenge. If this book touched you, inspired you, made you laugh, cry or scream – you now must pass it along. You can give your copy away, or go buy another one. You can read a story out loud, or paraphrase it as you remember it, I really don't care.

I wrote this book to make the world just a little better. With a little effort, you can be part of the team getting the job done.

Be sure to visit **thepennycollector.com** and join in the conversation. By the time you read this, there will be many more stories available to enjoy, but my hope is that my voice will be just one of many.

You have all been depositing pennies for years. It's time to check your balance and do a little shopping, or a lot.

SEE YOU AT THE MALL OF LIFE,

I'LL BE THE GUY WITH THE PENNY ON MY RUNNING SHOE